PORTRAITS FROM BEYOND

PORTRAITS FROM BEYOND

THE MEDIUMSHIP OF THE BANGS SISTERS

BY

N. RILEY HEAGERTY

Author of *The French Revelation*

WHITE CROW

www.whitecrowbooks.com

Portraits From Beyond

The Mediumship of the Bangs Sisters

All Non-Quoted Material in Text: Author/Editor: N.R. Heagerty

Copyright © 2016 by N. Riley Heagerty. All rights reserved.

Published and printed in the United States of America and the United Kingdom by White Crow Books; an imprint of White Crow Productions Ltd.

For information, contact White Crow Books
at 3 Hova Villas, Hove, BN3 3DH United Kingdom,
or e-mail to info@whitecrowbooks.com.

Cover Designed by Butterflyeffect
Interior design by Velin@Perseus-Design.com
Front cover image: "Ethel," courtesy and permission from Camp Chesterfield, Indiana.

Paperback ISBN 978-1-910121-65-8
eBook   ISBN 978-1-910121-66-5

Non Fiction / Body, Mind & Spirit / Spiritualism / Death & Dying

www.whitecrowbooks.com

To my Mother, Barbara Jane Heagerty, who entered the World of Spirits on 20, January 2014 & to my Father, John Heagerty, who is making his way to her.

A NOTE ABOUT THE
PHOTOS & PORTRAITS

I have traveled far and wide to obtain photos of the Bangs portraits for this book and many of them are not perfect but I would rather have them slightly imperfect and be included in the work rather than not include them.

In some images there are slight camera reflections (always a challenge), and shadows but I am hoping the reader will look beyond these this and enjoy the wondrous portraits of the Bangs Sisters as they are presented.

~ N. Riley Heagerty, 2016

1. Spirit Ethel, ibid. Camp Chesterfield, one of my favorites

ACKNOWLEDGEMENTS

I would like to thank Ron Nagy, the researcher and historian at Lily Dale for digging deep into the dusty old archives to find me many rare articles and research gems from the old Spiritualist publications to include in this work. He is a true comrade in the field of precipitated spirit portraits; Mike Tymn, the researcher and author for his inspiration as a writer; to Jon Beecher, the publisher of White Crow Books for believing in my work and the phenomena of the wondrous Bangs Sisters; to the many old, rare, used bookstores I have visited over the years and the gems I have found; to the following Spiritualist organizations for their permission to use photos of the spirit portraits: The Golden Gate Spiritualist Church, San Francisco; the Morris Pratt Institute, Wisconsin; Astara Spiritual Organization, California; Portsmouth Spiritualist Church, England; The Lily Dale Assembly, Lily Dale, NY; Chesterfield Spiritualist Camp, Indiana; Wonewoc Spiritualist Camp, Wisconsin; Harmony Grove Spiritualist Camp, California; to Mandi Shepp, Library Director, Marion H. Skidmore Library, Lily Dale, for painstakingly locating other valuable research items; to Shannon Taggert for her photography of some of the Lily Dale portraits; to the Spirits; to my animals, Midi Pantaloon (Country Belle), and Little Bittle and last but never least, my eternal Sweetheart, & wife, Caroline "Clem" Robertson, who has been with me, side by side, on the Good Red Road.

LIST OF ILLUSTRATIONS

—————➤●◄—————

1. Cover photo of Spirit "Ethel," courtesy of Camp Chesterfield, Indiana

2. Bangs in Black, late 1870's, Elizabeth left, May, right

3. Alex Mckee, precipitated in eight minutes in daylight, ibid. Camp Chesterfield

4. Iola, guide of Admiral Moore, from *Glimpses of the Next State* by Admiral Usborne Moore

5. Cleopatra, precipitated for Admiral Moore, courtesy, Portsmouth Spiritualist Church, England

6. William T. Stead, black and white photo of colored portrait, from *Dawn of the Awakened Mind*, by John S. King

7. Indian girl Blossom, full length, photo courtesy of The National Spiritualist Association of Churches (NSAC), Lily Dale

8. Dr. Sharp, spirit guide of one of America's most famous direct voice mediums, Etta Wriedt, ibid. Camp Chesterfield

9. Queen Victoria, full length portrait in all her splendor, ibid. Camp Chesterfield, precipitated for Dr. Carson of Kansas City

10. Audrey Alford, black and white photo of color portrait precipitated in 22 minutes at a demonstration in front of a large audience at Camp Chesterfield in 1911, from Photographing the Invisible by James Coates

CONTENTS

FOREWORD

In the Christian Bible there are detailed accounts of communication with spirits by clairvoyance; seeing spirits in their minds and then describing what they had seen. The medium is the connection between the living and the dead.

Many methods were used to contact the spirit world. The most outstanding example was Moses receiving the Ten Commandments written by the fingers of God. This was a fine example of psychography or more commonly known as slate writing in spiritualist language. In the mid 19th century, spirits produced knocks or raps on walls, floors, tables and ceilings. This phenomenon was refined by the Fox Sisters, Kate and Maggie on March 31, 1848 when a system of two way communication was established from the spirit of Charles Rosna. This date is known as the advent of Modern Spiritualism. Later developments brought slate writing, automatic writing and artwork; all were a means of communicating with spirits.

The Bangs Sisters, Elizabeth and May, were two of the most well-known physical mediums of the later 19th century and early 20th centuries. The sister's phenomena started when they were young girls quite unexpectedly when furniture would move and levitate and coal would appear in the room they were in from unseen forces. Later in their young lives they were caught up in the Spiritualist movement and began to experience and produce slate writing, automatic writing and art work—precipitated portraits that would appear on a blank canvas of the deceased during a séance. The portraits first appeared as a drab black and white image then, with practice, and as their powers increased, appeared in brilliant colors. The Bangs Sisters traveled from their home town of Chicago, Illinois to Chesterfield Indiana, and Lily Dale, New York across the United States to every major city and into the European Continent. The Bangs Sisters have been remembered most for their Precipitated Spirit Painting mediumship.

N. Riley Heagerty; spiritualist, author, researcher and friend, has compiled research from all known and obsolete journals, newspapers, books and archives across the United States and Europe to arrange all the available information concerning the Bangs Sisters that has ever been placed in one book. This work has been a work of obsession and love for the Religion of Spiritualism and the complete and fair evaluation of the Bangs Sisters. This book, the following pages, should be considered the definitive research book concerning the Bangs Sisters and related Spiritualist phenomena.

Ron Nagy, Historian,
Lily Dale, NY

INTRODUCTION

———⟫●⟪———

"Whatever the humblest men affirm from their own experience is always worth listening to, but what even the cleverest of men, in their ignorance deny, is never worth a moment's attention."

~ SIR WILLIAM BARRETT

It is an honor to have written this book concerning the Bangs Sisters and their phenomena. They have been a part of my life for many a year. My first published work about them was a lengthy serialized article within the British publication of the late Noah's Ark Society, *The Newsletter*, which ran in consecutive installment from January to November, 1997, and also later on in 2006, a lengthy article I did on the Bangs was published by *The Zerdin Buzzsheet*, the premier publication concerning physical mediumship, also in England. On the complete cover of two of the issues of the *Newsletter* and the one *Buzzsheet*, which was 8 x 12, were color photos of spirit precipitated portraits by the Bangs Sisters. I was truly honored. I have lectured in both America and England on the Bangs phenomena and the reaction from the audience is always the same: complete wonder and astonishment at the phenomena itself, then an amazed confusion at how they could not have known about these seemingly miraculous events before and, of course, the automatic response from some that it must be fraud because it is far too incredible to be true; simply too much for them to comprehend.

Historic American Spiritualism, the heyday of which this research-er would place between 1848 and 1948, does not reside within the mainstream of contemporary thought but, if we were living in Chicago or, better yet, the famous Spiritualist towns of Camp Chesterfield, Indiana, or Lily Dale, New York, in the year say, 1909, we most certainly would have heard of the famous Bangs Sisters but alas, we are not. An in-depth look at the lives and phenomena of these two mediums was necessary. This is, in my opinion, the only way that a fair, intelligent and reasoned balance can be attained in understanding the authentic records of Modern Spiritualism and Mediumship. Just peeking below the surface with these matters is not enough. One must dive deep to find the pearls.

My first book, *The French Revelation*, was a rescue operation, saving from a certain march into obscurity and oblivion the séance records contained within the rare, out of print books and unpublished material of Edward C. Randall and his work with one of the greatest American independent voice mediums,[1] Emily S. French. That work was published as a complete edition. Mrs. French's mediumship was without controversy, with the exception of a report filed by Dr. Isaac K. Funk[2] (1839-1912), and this was, in turn, recanted by himself when he, predeceasing Mrs. French by one year, manifested of all things, at one of her last séances, speaking in his own voice. The Bangs Sisters story, which is also a complete work, is more complicated and their phenomena of independent writing and most notably, their precipitated spirit portraits, were prone to attacks, some from individuals with names of distinction, such as Hereward Carrington (1880-1958)[3] the British psychic investigator and author, and David P. Abbott (1863-1934)

---

[1] Spirit voices speaking independently of the medium, seemingly out of thin air, recognized by the sitters, and able to hold conversations since they can also hear besides speak.

[2] Isaac K. Funk, *The Psychic Riddle*, 1907; see also N. Riley Heagerty's, *The French Revelation*, 2005, Pt.3, Chap.11, Emily French Solves the Psychic Riddle: The Return of Dr. Isaac K. Funk. Dr. Funk knew what he witnessed with Mrs. French was highly evidential and genuine, but left loopholes in his findings. He stated at that séance {speaking from the spirit world} with Mrs. French—after being told by Edward Randall that he had failed at the crucial moment to publish the truth which could have helped humanity— "I realize that now more than ever. It is a fact that I was afraid of the criticism of men of science. I now regret very much that I did not fully publish my conclusions. In my own mind there was no doubt."

[3] Hereward Carrington, *Personal Experiences in Spiritualism*, 1918

the amateur magician, inventor and author.[4] One need only read the well-researched but amplified-article by Teller and Todd Karr: " David P. Abbott and the Notorious Bangs Sisters" to understand how the press of the day, around 1905-1909, mainly the *Chicago Daily Tribune* and the *Washington Post*,[5] were openly hostile towards these mediums. Within my own research, I have found that the highly evidential reports of the Bangs phenomena, when looked at closely and balanced within the court of common sense, by far and away, outweigh the negative, jaundiced reports. The reports of fraud, being somewhat boisterous and rabid, but few—pale in comparison with eyewitness reports of individuals of unimpeachable character that crush those negative theories and accusations, no matter how aggressive or intellectually elaborate they were, into dust. Scandalous character assassinations, just as much now as then, generate more headlines. David P. Abbott, early on, referred to the Bangs precipitated spirit portraits as: "The most remarkable mediumistic performance ever given to the world," but naturally assumed, like most of the conjuring fraternity, of which he was an amateur, that if any form of physical phenomena manifesting in a séance could be duplicated by magic, then it conclusively proved fraud on the part of the mediums. These belligerent, crass assumptions, stated publicly—and which did, I am sure, unmask fraudulent mediums in certain cases, and all the better for it—were the standard mode of operation for the critics of the day. Like a terrorist who throws a rock, then runs like a coward, we have examples such as Mr. Abbott who wrote: *"The Spirit Portrait Mystery: Its Final Solution,"* but, did Mr. Abbott actually sit in the presence of the Bangs Sisters for a precipitated spirit portrait and actually witness what he said and what he based his theories on? We shall see. This has been examined in total within this work along with another "sensational expose" published in 1901[6] by an English investigator of psychic phenomena, Reverend Stanley L. Krebs, entitled: *"A Description of Some Trick Methods Used by Miss Bangs of Chicago."* Also, the necessary reports of Hereward Carrington, mentioned above, have been included.

The book is illustrated, with numerous photographs of Bangs precipitated spirit portraits I have located, and many black and white photos

[4] David P. Abbott, *The Spirit Portrait Mystery; Its Final Solution*, 1913

[5] Teller and Todd Karr, *House of Mystery: The Magic Science of David P. Abbott*, 2005

[6] *Journal of the Society for Psychical Research*, England, 1901

of others from rare books. Many portraits and photos, unfortunately, had no written history with them to give us an idea of when or where they were precipitated, and for whom. There were, over the course of the Bangs career, hundreds and hundreds, better yet, thousands of precipitated portraits done. Many have been lost to the ages, or could be sitting in attics or basements, collecting dust and, I am sure, many have been unknowingly and sadly, consigned to the trash heap. In one astounding instance, which took place in January 1910, the Bangs Sisters had put on an exhibition in Kansas City of over one hundred precipitated spirit portraits and allegorical scenes of the spirit world. Dr. C. H. Carson, who arranged the announcement, said: "Nothing before seen can compare with the marvelous beauty of these psychic pictures and creations from an unseen world." (See Chap.3) I am looking out the window as I write this, shaking my head in wonderment at where those portraits could be and trying to imagine what it must have been like to witness: the easels, a hundred of them situated throughout the hall; the colors of the event, and the turn of the century vernacular and dress. I have traveled far and have corresponded with experts[7] to obtain photos, including England, California, Wisconsin, Indiana and New York. My friend, Ron Nagy, the historian and researcher at Lily Dale, New York, knows and understands the great mystery surrounding the whereabouts of Bangs portraits. His important work is discussed in the Appendices and is quoted at certain times throughout this book. As far as this work, I had to conclude my search so I could get the book published otherwise I could probably have spent the rest of my life searching for these elusive gems. For someone like myself who never likes to give up, this was tough, but necessary. I would also like to say that I encourage everyone who reads this work to take the time to go and see for yourself the Bangs portraits at Lily Dale and at the Hett Memorial Art Museum at Camp Chesterfield. Knowing something of the history of them makes seeing them all the more incredible and you will know exactly what I mean when you see them up close.

I am compelled to do research on the great, early mediums because I feel that the modern world, thanks to outdated religious concepts and scientific bias, has been kept woefully unaware of phenomenal events that have happened within the great century between 1848 and 1948 which, in thousands of reported instances through mediumship, positively prove life after death and spirit communication. My so-called mission statement (if

---

[7]   Ron Nagy, Lily Dale historian and author of *Slate Writing*, 2009, *Precipitated Spirit Paintings*, 2010, and *The Spirits of Lily Dale*, 2011, Galde Press.

there ever was one) of why I do this research was instigated in many respects by the following facts. In certain instances involving reports of the Near Death Experience (NDE), the individual who has temporarily died and has gone to the world of spirits is met by a guide who, after hearing the plea by the person to continue in their new life in spirit rather than go back to the earth again, simply states to the individual, "Now that we have talked about your ongoing need to keep going here in this wondrous new life, tell me..." the guide now asks, "What have you done for mankind?" Many individuals do not know how to answer that simple but profound question and then decide that the only reasonable thing they can do is go back to earth and exact some kind of change, on whatever level, that aids to the moral or physical uplifting of humanity. This affected how I saw doing this research work and publishing the results. It is something, to me, *that just might help humanity*, however great or small, and possibly raise its spiritual consciousness. The world should be allowed to have access to the past records of what took place with so many of the great pioneer mediums. It is part of history and should not be consigned to the dark hole of obscurity. Truth always finds its way and, in this case, I don't mind helping it do so.

By compiling this material, and editing it into one all-inclusive edition (everything available that I could find), it will make accessible to the reader an abundance of rare spirit precipitated portraits, all of which are more than 110-120 years old, and authentic eye-witness accounts and reports of one of the most stupendous events that has ever manifested within the records of Historic American Spiritualism: the phenomenal Bangs Sisters. What was once hidden in obscurity can now live again. The night brings forth the stars.

N. Riley Heagerty, 2014

CHAPTER 1

THE BANGS SISTERS
Essential Collected Material & Perspectives

———————⟫●⟪———————

"The advent of Spiritualism is through facts and not theories. Its purpose is positive knowledge."

~ HUDSON TUTTLE

From what I can have gathered in my research, it appears that the Bangs were mediums at birth, meaning that their powers unfolded accordingly as time went on and they were instructed in their development by their spirit guides, chiefly a Captain W. Stevens who manifested later on as they got older. This is not surprising as far as mediumistic development. The mid 19th century mediums The Davenport Brothers, Ira and William, the sensational physical mediums of Buffalo, New York and the equally astounding Eddy Brothers, William and Horatio (and family), of Vermont, were already developed as they took their first mortal breaths. Phenomena attended the Eddy children in their cradles and when the Davenport boys (and, I want to add, Libby, their little sister, who was also a powerhouse of mediumistic force) sat for the first time for manifestations joined by their parents at their tea table in 1855, the foundation of the house shook and the crockery fell

1

from the shelves smashing to the floor and, according to Mr. and Mrs. Davenport, physical phenomena had been manifesting in their home years before that event on a nightly basis while the children slept. It has been documented that phenomena were happening in the Bangs house when the children were very young, and the family did sit often for manifestations.[1]

May and Elizabeth were both born in Chicago to Edward and Meroe Bangs who were originally from Maine. May was born in 1862 and Lizzie, as she was called, in 1859. They had two brothers, Edward and William, and there is no legitimate documentation of them having had any mediumistic gifts. Mr. Bangs, it was said, was a tinsmith and stove repairman by trade and the mother attended to the family. As stated in one source, she was also a medium but this was never legitimately verified. Elizabeth was married in 1877 to John Paul, had two girls, and was divorced in 1888. May was married in 1884 to William D. Gausden, had one son, and eventually divorced. She was married again at least two times and the press had a field day with all of the marital drama surrounding one of the famous "spook" mediums. One scandal-infested report came from the *New York Times* dated July 1st, 1915 concerning a wealthy gentleman, Jacob Lesher, who had married May Bangs in 1907. It said that the medium, "...proposed to him three times before he was finally won over by the assurance that the spirit of Lesher's mother was urging the match and that he himself *would become 25 years younger and would never again be ill.*" Some of the more colorful headlines and reporting of the day were:

"MAY BANGS AND HER MOTHER ARRESTED FOR DOING BUSINESS WITHOUT A LICENSE" *Atchinson Little Globe,* 1881

May Bangs and her mother, now reportedly living in Chicago, had been arrested for doing business without a license. The pair argued that they were evangelists and that such a charge could not be made against a minister.

"SPOOKS GO ON A STRIKE" *Chicago Daily Tribune,* 1891.

---

[1] There is a rare, interesting article written in this work by the mother, Meroe Bangs, concerning the early family sittings.

In the early 1890's, according to the Kerr article mentioned in the introduction, a Chicago grand jury attempted to indict the Bangs Sisters but failed due to technicalities, according to the (*Chicago Daily Tribune*, March 7, 1890). In 1891, a bill was passed by the Illinois Senate prohibiting anyone from personating the spirits of the dead, commonly known as spirit-medium séances, on penalty of fine and imprisonment (*Chicago Daily Tribune*, May 16, 1891). At least one Chicago spiritualist blamed the Bangs Sisters for this new law, saying that although "they were gifted with unearthly powers, their greed for gold had led them to abuse it."

"A RUINED MAN: INVENTOR YOST, THE PREY OF THE MEDIUMS" *Los Angeles Times*, 1895.

Yost supposedly had sittings with the Bangs for communications through a typewriter, which was indeed an early manifestation[2] that was taking place with them. There was no official indication that the messages were not genuine, but Yost's continued, insatiable need to sit with other mediums, *it* was said, led to his alleged financial ruin.

"SPIRIT PAINTINGS BAFFLE POLICE: DETECTIVES VISIT HOME OF THE BANGS SISTERS WITH EVELYN CAMPBELL - SEARCH DISCLOSES NO TRICKERY" *The Sunflower*, 1900

Quoting Evelyn Campbell: "Well, in whatever way the Bangs Sisters produce those pictures, there is no sign of trickery in their house or furniture."

Detective Sergeant George Trafton was speaking—Sergeant Trafton, known as one of the shrewdest detectives on the police force of Chicago. "We were coming down the steps of the beautiful home at 654 West Adams Street, where the Bangs Sisters produce spirit paintings, (over) which such a controversy has raged since it was rumored that Dr. I. K. Funk, millionaire publisher and philanthropist

---

[2]   As described by Quaestor Vitae in *LIGHT*, one of the oldest and most famous English Spiritualist weekly publications, dated January 25th, 1896, in describing one of the most spectacular demonstrations of 'direct-writing' by Miss Lizzie Bangs, "..the machine kept on working when held up in the air by four of the men present. The hand which had done the work also materialized." See Chapter Two, "Independent Slate Writing."

of New York City, had paid $1,500 for a painting. Charges of fraud have been freely made by other mediums against the Bangs Sisters. In answer to this the sisters invited the fullest police inspection of their home. So it was that inspector Wheeler of the Desplains Street Station sent detective Sergeant Trafton upon an investigation trip to the home of the Sisters.

The article said:

"FINDS NO SIGNS OF TRICKERY"

I was permitted to accompany him, and we went through the house from top to the bottom, inspecting every cranny and crevice, every room, ceiling, floor, cupboard and drawer.

We found nothing of a suspicious nature, no slits in the floor, no false panels, no cabinets—nothing that would aid in any trickery. We especially examined the floors and walls of the small room in which the sisters always "materialize" the pictures, and the room directly above, beneath, and each side of it. "There is nothing here," said Detective Sergeant Trafton. "I used to be a carpenter before I went on the force and I know when the floor or ceiling has been disturbed. There not only is nothing here now but neither floors have been disturbed or replaced for years."

"It is too cruel," said Mrs. Bangs as she showed us through the house, "the manner in which we are being persecuted. Just because we hold aloof from those cheap mediums, many of whom are fakers, they are saying these things about us."

"Dr. Funk himself is satisfied," said Miss Minnie Bangs. "Here is the beautiful dictionary he sent us for Christmas, and here are the letters he wrote us before we sent the framed pictures to him. These do not look as if he discredited us, do they?"

(Dr. Isaac Kauffman Funk was the director and principal proprietor of the prestigious publishing house Funk & Wagnalls, New York.)

"BANGS SISTERS INTEREST POLICE" *Chicago Daily Tribune*, 1905

According to this article, one reader wisely pointed out that the sisters can't produce a picture of a relative of the sitter without a photograph, no matter what they may say to the contrary. They have to obtain these photos either in an underhanded manner or with the consent of the sitter. If they have no photo, well, it's a case of "unfavorable conditions."

The reader can decide for themselves what they believe as far as the Bangs Sisters and any photographs involved in the precipitation process in Part 3.

"HOW GHOSTS PAINT SPIRIT PORTRAITS" *Chicago Daily Tribune*, 1905

A local printer, it was stated in this article, proposed that the blank canvas that was used at the beginning of the precipitation sitting, was *"switched under one of the sister's skirts*, for a prepared painting wrapped in several layers of tissue that could be progressively removed to make the portrait gradually appear."

A Kansas City minister, A. T. Osborne, according to the Todd Karr article mentioned above, told *the New York Times* that an explanation of the Bangs' portraits had come to him in a dream ('Solves' Spirit Paintings, July 9, 1908). Osborne's theory was that "They made a magic-lantern slide...the portrait was thrown on a blank canvas by means of a stereopticon. A dissolving-view device caused the picture to fade from the blank. The painted enlargement was slipped on the trick table and a cover whisked off the moment the magic lantern view vanished."

Confident that Osborne's method was ridiculous and puerile beyond words, the Bangs Sisters promptly telegrammed the minister and offered him $1000 if he could correctly demonstrate the secret of their portraits. When Osborne accepted, they sent another telegram demanding that the Reverend wager $1000 as well. (*The Washington Post* "Girls Seek Pastor's Coin," July 11, 1908) reported Osborne's reaction: "Of course I can't have anything to do with such a proposal. I can't do any betting, and whoever heard of a minister with $1000?"

An individual, Mrs. F Cushman, heard that Osborne had said the following about the spirit portraits: "It's easy and perfectly simple, it is done by the influence of mind and, by that niche, there is absolutely nothing supernatural about the work. The picture that is handed to you is not the picture of the person who is dead..."

Mrs. Cushman: "That is not so," (after having secured a picture of her dead sister) "they do not make the changes. They didn't in mine, and I never heard of them doing it before. The Bangs Sisters never knew my sister. They did not even know her first name. They had never seen a picture of her because I have the only one in existence."

Another win for the Bangs Sisters.

On a more harmonious note, this next article concerns the early lives and phenomena of the mediums.

The National Spiritualist, July 1ˢᵗ, 1940

Who were these miracle-working women? Born of a typical American family named Bangs, they were reared in average American surroundings. These sisters, Lizzie and May, were scarcely past toddling age when they began astonishing the neighborhood with phenomena of a very unusual sort. Pieces of coal falling seemingly from the ceiling to the floor of their home. Coal that bore no similarity whatsoever to any ever seen in the surrounding country was one of the first visible instances of the strange power. By their fourth or fifth year spirit rappings, voices from the world beyond, and the moving of heavy pieces of furniture by invisible forces were within their grasp.

Strange, indeed, for girls scarcely past babyhood, and certainly beyond comprehension of childish minds. They must have suffered more than their share of qualms at their difference from girls of the same age.

Physical manifestations, such as the materialization of hands, automatic writing, independent slate writing, full-form etherialization, clairvoyance and clairaudience were by now almost daily occurrences. Within the next few years an even more remarkable ability was demonstrated by the sisters. Something no medium had ever achieved before: spirit communication by typewriter. Later, when word of the spirit paintings got out, Lizzie and May Bangs were now famous.

The new power baffled the keenest intellects. The portraits reproduced were the work of high order as well as excellent likenesses. The conditions under which the paintings were made precluded all possibility of deception. When one considers that an artist would require at least five hours to produce even a poor portrait, the fact that the Bangs portraits only required from thirty minutes to three hours becomes more astounding. (In time, as the precipitation power developed, the portraits were done in minutes. -ED)

The story of the paintings and the history of the Bangs girls were headlined in papers and magazines throughout the country. Fakirs and magicians tried to imitate the performance. They came, were unmasked, and passed in steady procession. Skeptics reversed their opinions and wrote favorable notices. Meanwhile the sisters carried on quietly and serenely, unmoved by the storm raging around them. Such headlines as: "The Facts of Immortality Verified" left them unmoved. They had a job to do and did it.

Caring nothing for the pomps and vanities of this world, they wasted no precious time on shams. They lived comfortably but simply. Their lives were dedicated to helping others: the needy, the sick in body and soul. With only a strand of hair, or perhaps a message locked tight between slates—mute pleas of supplication from aching hearts—to help them, the sisters were able to bring what had seemed forever gone into the light of day. Countless were the thousands who received comfort and happiness in this way.

Many famous men and women who traveled to their doors to criticize, left singing hymns of praise.

The residences in Chicago that would become their home base were, according to their own program ads, 645 West Adams Street and 3 South Elizabeth St., Chicago; Hedrick Cottage at Camp Chesterfield, and various addresses at Lily Dale. I checked on Global Mapping to see if any of the Bangs residences were left in the hopes of going to Chicago to photograph them for the book but none were there; they were long ago lost to the ages.

There are two famous Spiritualist communities, mentioned above, where the Bangs Sisters held residences, on and off, for more than 30 years. These were Lily Dale, south of Buffalo in Western New York, and Camp Chesterfield, Chesterfield, Indiana, in Madison County in the east-central area of that state. Each of these communities, even now in the present day, hosts thousands of visitors, especially during their 'season', which usually lasts from July to September.

Elizabeth Bangs passed from this life on February 27th, 1920. The mother of the Bangs, Meroe, passed on November 22nd, 1917 and, both Bangs sisters appeared in the Nationalist Spiritualist Association Convention souvenir book of 1922 as famous Spiritualists who had passed on. But the mystery of May Bangs has been solved. Both she and Elizabeth are buried in Forest Home Cemetery, in Chicago.

Since I have made mention of the famous Spiritualist community, Camp Chesterfield, it is necessary at this point in the narrative to present an astounding event that occurred there on the evening of the 30th August, 1908, reported by the *Nuncie Morning Star* newspaper. I have also combined that, with a report compiled and written by Irene Swann, who was in 1969 the curator of the Hett Memorial Art Gallery & Museum, situated at that camp, that published a small booklet entitled: *"The Bangs Sisters and their Precipitated Spirit Portraits."* It was reported that this was the Bangs' first public demonstration for this wondrous phenomenon. I will also include sections from my own article that was published in 1997. This is one of many definitive examples of the power of these mediums, which obliterates the fraud theories that indicated that the Bangs portraits were painted beforehand.

CAMP CHESTERFIELD AUDITORIUM, INDIANA (This was actually the second auditorium, built in 1903; the first one, a large tent, was built in 1891)

It was August, 1908, that a large audience filled to capacity the auditorium at the world famous Spiritualist community, Camp Chesterfield in the state of Indiana, USA. They had come to witness a demonstration of psychic power; one of the most unique and marvelous in the world.

On a table set in the middle of the stage, a select committee had placed a blank, standard size canvas, which was minutely examined and said to have no markings or painting of any kind, nor signs of chemical treatment. Behind the canvas was placed a coal-oil lamp. The canvas remained in position in full view of the audience until the developed portrait was completed. Upon entering the auditorium, each person was given a ticket, the numbered stub of which was placed into a vat and then, when the entire audience had finished this process, one stub was drawn randomly from the collection and the number read aloud. The ticket belonged to a Mr. and Mrs. Alford, a prominent family of

Marion, Indiana, who were then invited to take a seat on the stage. The mediums then entered the stage and sat down, never touching the canvas or approaching it. After a few moments a thin, vapor-like cloud or shadow swept across the canvas and then disappeared. The audience sat rigidly, their eyes tense and fixed on the stage. Once again, another wave of mist seemed to float and pulsate across the canvas and it also vanished. The other world artist, it seemed, was making preliminary sketches and trying out different color schemes. Soon the outline bust form of a person began to appear in the center of the canvas, features becoming more distinct along with the hair and face and, slowly, the entire form of a young girl was clearly distinguishable for all to see. The eyes on the portrait *were closed*. Suddenly, in a flash, the eyes opened and the audience cheered. The entire process took about twenty minutes and, when completed, the picture was handed around the auditorium for inspection.

Mr. Alford, clearly shaken, stood and announced that he and his wife were visiting Chesterfield for the first time. They were not Spiritualists in belief but, most certainly, the form on the canvas, which he pointed to, was the exact likeness of their young daughter, Audrey. Mrs. Alfred had worn around her neck, hidden from sight, a locket containing a photograph of their daughter almost duplicate in likeness to the picture obtained. The Bangs had not seen the locket picture or any photo of the child. I have included three photos of Audrey Alford. One is from the Hett Art Gallery at Camp Chesterfield, which I have seen and examined up close; one is a close-up, and the other has come from a rare book by James Coates. It is the only verifiable proof, and photograph, I have ever seen of a precipitated portrait, which had actually changed in appearance, which was quite common with Bangs paintings. The one photo in black and white, shows the finished work from the public demonstration at Chesterfield with Audrey wearing a teardrop necklace and a spray of flowers, or corsage on her dress. The color photo shows the portrait, after having been donated to Camp Chesterfield years later by a member of the Alford family without the necklace and corsage. They apparently having been originally precipitated on to the original work just for the mother and then dematerialized when it was donated. How truly marvelous.

In researching these mediums, three things initially and not surprisingly stand out. First, like the majority of the most powerful and famous physical mediums from America, many of whom were some of the highest ranking in Spiritualism (see Appendices), the Bangs Sisters lived and developed their many gifts within the Great Lakes region of the North eastern United States. There was, seemingly, a zone of electrical energy in this section of the country said by the spirits themselves to be perfect for the manifestations of physical phenomena due to the great bodies of water and the dry, crisp atmosphere. The Bangs' hometown of Chicago, Illinois, is situated right on Lake Michigan. Secondly, that they were siblings, giving us a definitive example of a genetically connected powerhouse of mediumistic force. A few other examples of names mentioned earlier were the Eddy Brothers and the Davenport Brothers and others come to mind: the Fox Sisters, the Berry Sisters, the Jonathan Koons family and the Misses Dunsmore, and there are others. Thirdly, in the case of the Bangs Sisters, there is not a single complete and definitive book written about their lives and phenomena, with the exception of an outstanding small book written by my fellow researcher, Ron Nagy, entitled *Precipitated Spirit Portraits*, which covers the Bangs in condensed form and also the only other mediums of that time that manifested spirit portraits, The Campbell Brothers. Ron is the recognized authority on the science, chemistry and history of precipitated spirit portraits. Also, there is the Irene Swann pamphlet mentioned earlier and a small booklet, published in 1986, called *Chesterfield Lives, 1886-1986, Our First Hundred Years* published by Camp Chesterfield. Both are also outstanding.

ELECTRICAL CONDITIONS AND MANIFESTATIONS

Concerning the electrical conditions around the Great Lakes, there is a very interesting and somewhat terse and futuristically prophetic quote from Vice-Admiral W. Usborne Moore, (1850-1918), dated February 10th, 1911:

> Curious it is that, while the great secret of the knowledge of immortal life is to be found around the Great Lakes of North America, where the natural electrical conditions are so favorable to all forms of physical manifestations, the people are, on this subject, the most ignorant, intolerant, and bigoted on the face of the civilized earth. With nine men out of ten, to mention the occult is to provoke a sneer; in this respect it is worse there now than it was in England sixty years ago. The motive of life is the chase of the almighty dollar; materialism is rampant and, as far as I could see, there is no reason to hope for any improvement for very many years to come.

SEEING THE BANGS SISTERS' PRECIPITATED PORTRAITS

To this date, I have personally examined up close more than thirty Bangs Sisters' portraits, including twenty-six which are exhibited at the Hett Gallery at Chesterfield and at least eight at Lily Dale. Some are full length in frames that are 60 x 40 inches, and I can only wonder what the experience must have been like for the individuals who sat with these mediums to witness a manifestation of this level.

"Startling and marvellous" would be mild characterizations when describing these works of spirit art. Most of the portraits were produced before color photography came into being and this only adds to the wonder because many of them appear, right now, to have the clarity of a photograph. That is until one looks closely, and sees that it goes beyond this, way beyond. No hands ever touched these portraits when they were precipitated, and there are no brush strokes to be seen. The eyes especially, with the irises of various colors, have a transcendent beauty about them; a clear almost illuminated gaze that one never forgets when experienced. Many people have claimed that the eyes on certain portraits seemed to follow them as they walked around the room and I myself can attest to this with the portrait of "Clara" displayed at Lily Dale, which is illustrated later in the book.[3] The hair in most of the portraits is in detail down to the most miniscule strands, waves, colors, top knots and styles. Ringlets, braids, long luxurious flowing tresses and curling tendrils can be seen. There are elaborate dresses, suits, silks and Indian robes, delicate veils, lace, turbans, blouses, brilliant white dress shirts and neckties, majestic long flowing beards and stylish moustaches, necklaces, ruby red lips, turquoise, rings, cameos and other forms of gorgeous jewelry and decorations; threaded seams, stitch work designs, intricate knots, exquisite pearls, bracelets, beads and buttons; vegetation such as red and white roses and other flowers, carved marble, and other flourishes of artistic beauty. The colors, most notably in the faces, are life-like and fresh and seem to have never faded; they look as if they were precipitated yesterday. The only comparison, it has been said, to these splendid works would be to the classical Renaissance artist, Raphael, and the Dutch master, Rembrandt. There is a spirit quote in this work which refers to this in Part 3.

---

[3] The Lily Dale Historian, Ron Nagy, has stated that no subject in an authentic Bangs portrait will have discernible eyelashes.

From what I have found, the actual material used by the spirit artists and chemists has never been scientifically proven to be any known substance used by conventional artists.

The portraits have been examined by art experts over the years and they cannot explain the media used. The portraits are not oils, watercolors, pastels, ink, crayon, charcoal or anything else. The material looked to me like fine dust, as fragile looking as dry cigar ash that has been ground into your hand. It has also been compared to tempera watercolor. Another description of modern day is the word airbrush and, although it seems adequate, it is one of those easy off the tongue words and, to this researcher, a highly inferior description. I have wondered how the material was precipitated: was it through the back of the canvas or on to the front? In one of the more fitting and historic statements describing the media used it was said that it looked like the fine dust of a butterfly's wings. How beautiful.

An excerpt from *The Bangs Sisters and their Precipitated Spirit Portraits*, issued as a small booklet in 1969 by Camp Chesterfield says:

> The precipitated spirit pictures are from eighty to ninety-five years old, and have withstood time very well. Many of the portraits were hung in the old Auditorium and hotels at Camp Chesterfield for many years, and these buildings did not have heat in the winter months. Many sitters stored pictures in attics and basements, and the colors are as beautiful now as the day they were executed.
>
> These outstanding works of art are the sitters relatives, friends, or guides who have passed on, with the exception of one portrait where the sitter appeared on a canvas with his twin daughters and wife, who were deceased.[4]
>
> The persons who sat for the spirit pictures were requested to bring a photograph of the departed, but were not asked to produce it. The portraits were not copies of the concealed photograph. When completed, the facial resemblance was amazing, and the color tones often grew richer and deeper.
>
> Many of the portraits changed when taken home. The hair on some would be altered to look as it had when the subject was on earth. A

---

[4] *Dr. Daugherty, from Camp Chesterfield Portraits*

few blouses and dresses changed to seem more familiar, and in several cases the eyes would open and close. In one portrait of a spirit guide, pearls appeared around the neck a few days later when the sitter said the girl always wore them. In another full-length picture, more flowers appeared on a rose bush.

The gift of precipitated portraits by the Bangs did not begin until the autumn of 1894. During the early periods of the girls' development, it was necessary to curtain the canvas, or place it in a dark chamber, and several sittings were required to complete the picture. As the gift developed, Elizabeth and May were able to demonstrate the phenomenon in full light.

Initially, the portraits were produced as follows: two identical paper mounted canvases were placed together, face to face, and then leaned up against a window, the lower ends of the canvases resting upon a table situated right in front of the window. (See photo gallery).

Each sister would sit on one side of the table and pinch the canvases together with one hand. The window curtains would be drawn up close to the frames on the top and either side. This procedure was arranged so that the only light coming into the room itself was through the canvases, which were translucent.

The sitter(s), in most cases, would sit at the end of the table, directly opposite from the canvases facing them and, by doing so, intently watch the entire process, including the mediums, from start to finish. After a short time, the outline of shadows would begin to appear and disappear, the invisible artist testing color schemes and making preliminary sketches and then, usually at a somewhat rapid pace, the portrait would come into full view. When the frames were separated afterwards, the spirit portrait would be found on the surface of one of the canvases; usually the one nearest the sitter. In the earlier days, though the precipitated material was somewhat greasy to the touch, it left no stain on the other, non-precipitated canvas. Later on, the portraits were precipitated using the mysterious dust-like material mentioned above and, in many cases, only one canvas was used. Some took as little as five to eight minutes to complete.

In a letter written to Mr. James Coates, Ph.D., dated 17th September, 1910 and published in his book,[5] May Bangs, describing the process of precipitation said:

---

[5] *James Coates, Ph., D. F.A.S., Photographing the Invisible, London, L.N.Fowler & Co. 1911.*

13

The room is shaded sufficiently to cause all light from the window to pass through the canvas, thus enabling the sitter to witness the development and detect the least change in the shadows.

No two sittings are exactly alike. Usually in the development of a portrait the outer edges of the canvas become shadowed, showing different delicately colored lines, until the full outline of the head and shoulders is seen. When the likeness is sufficiently distinct to be recognized, the hair, drapery, and other decorations appear. In many cases, after the entire portrait is finished, the eyes gradually open, giving a lifelike appearance to the whole face.

This is a rare hand-written letter describing a very early precipitation sitting.

To *the Light of Truth* Spiritualist Periodical
From Dr. Carpenter, Olin, Iowa
Saturday, June 20, 1896

On April 25, 1896, I wrote a letter to the Bangs Sisters, of No. 3 South Elizabeth Street, Chicago, Illinois, to have them ask their guide, Capt. W. Stevens, to ascertain through my wife in spirit life if she could and would give me her picture. On the morning of May 9th I received an answer saying that if I would go there the week of May 10th, she would do so. Accordingly, on the 12th I went to the above named mediums in Chicago, Illinois. The 13th I spent in having canvas prepared and had a box made 24/30 inches in which I put prepared canvas. Not, however, before I carefully examined and marked same so I could fully identify it. I then nailed it securely shut. The box was then placed under a table leaning against the wall in which position it remained, the mediums sitting at one end of the table and myself at the other. After sitting from 10 minutes past 10 o'clock am until 10 minutes past one pm, the mediums held the slate under the table and received this message, "We have exhausted your patience, open the box."

We accordingly opened the box and to my great surprise and joy beheld a complete life sized picture of my wife and child in the spirit world. The picture is so natural and life-like that many of my neighbors and friends fully recognize it although they have been in spirit life for 33 years.

Of special note with this sitting was the fact that there was only one of the Bangs Sisters present, and although Dr. Carpenter requested a portrait of his wife, his child also manifested, most likely as a gift from the spirit artists. There is another example of this 'add-on' precipitation in Chapter 3. These early sittings, where the canvases were out of sight and in control of the sitter, suggested the possibility of them using a fraudulent procedure even though, in the case of Dr. Carpenter, he was sitting right there, and had controlled the entire process from beginning to end. The Bangs enemies and critics would pounce on each and every little possibility of trickery. With the advent of their broad daylight precipitations, it quieted the critics, but certainly not all.

Excerpt from *The Light of Truth*
The Light of Truth Publishing Company
Columbus, Ohio 1897

Lizzie and May Bangs, of 3 South Elizabeth Street, Chicago, Illinois are mediums of various phases, receiving spirit tests through clairvoyance, slate writing, typewriting, materialization, and later in the form of oil paintings. They have had many a battle with skeptics, but the phenomena occurring in their presence invariably made them the victors. Facts need no augmentation.

Bangs Sisters Advertisement
The Sunflower
July 15th, 1900

We desire to announce to our friends and numerous patrons that we will be at Lily Dale July 1st, and remain throughout the season.

We will occupy Mr. Huff's cottage on Melrose Park near the entrance, and open up our parlors with a fine collection of artwork superior to any heretofore exhibited. We will, as usual, give independent slate and paper writings, but will make a specialty of spirit portrait work in which attractive features in new lines of development cannot fail to be satisfactory to your patrons. Most of our work is now produced in broad sunlight, the form, features, and various tints gradually appearing to the eye of the sitter making a perfect portrait of the one whose likeness is desired.

The Lily Dale Chronicle
1900-20

Strolling about the grounds one is confronted by numerous signs before the doors such as BANGS SISTERS, phenomenal mediums, SPIRIT PORTRAITS a speciality.

The art galleries of the Bangs Sisters …are simply beautiful beyond description. The art of these mediums in producing spirit portraits is phenomenal. One sits with the portrait of a deceased friend in their pocket, and within thirty minutes the picture is transferred on canvas before their eyes. First comes the outline then gradually the picture develops. If you say the eyes are too light, they will change to the required color. The Bangs Sisters told the writer that under certain conditions they could get a spirit portrait of a person in spirit life that never had a likeness taken, by the sitter holding the looks of their friend in their mind. However, the imagination must apply much to make a natural picture. Also one sitting for their own picture will have three to fourteen spirit friends on the background of the photo.

Letter writing and slate writing are also a phenomenon; it is evident that some agency is employed other than the sleight of hand. By placing a gold watch on one corner of the slate, the writing will be done in gold, or using a silver dollar, the same, the writing will be in silver letters.

Chesterfield Camp Program
1909

THE BANGS SISTERS: PROGRAM

We desire to call the attention of our numerous friends and patrons, all interested in Spirit Art, to our special arrangements for Chesterfield Camp for the coming year of 1909.

We shall be in attendance as early as July 22, and remain throughout the season.

We will give daily attention to Independent Paper Writing communications and Spirit Portraiture.

We shall have on exhibition in our parlors a variety of beautiful art productions of elaborate design, exquisite texture and delicate tints, and prepared to give several sizes of painting at reasonable prices.

Our Independent Writing is given above board and in the broad daylight, under conditions that cannot fail to convince the most skeptical. In our Art Work, Portraits of loved ones gradually develop into life-like colors before the eyes of the sitter in a well-lighted window.

Through the agency of Departed Intelligences, we have recently invented a "Table Telephone," so sensitive to sound that Spirit Voices and Whispers can be distinctly heard and recognized while sitting in the light. This phase we will introduce this season at Camp Chesterfield in connection with Independent Writing Sittings.

Those desiring Portraits of departed friends should arrange time for sittings in advance, thereby avoiding disappointment and waiting.

Do Not Wait Until the Last of the Season When All Are Rushed, but COME EARLY.

Your patronage is respectfully solicited.
BANGS SISTERS
Home Address 645, W. Adams St.
Chicago
Hendrick Cottage
Chesterfield

The Religio-Philosophical Journal

This is an early eye-witness account of the Bangs children, dated 1871, from the book, *Nineteenth Century Miracles*, by Mrs. Emma Hardinge Britten.[6] Additionally, a very rare, written report from Meroe Bangs,

---

6   Emma Hardinge Britten (1823-1899), inspirational speaker and medium,

the mother of the Bangs Sisters. It is a gem, which clarifies in detail the early, mysterious manifestations at their home. The portents of mediumship:

The Children Mediums

We have on three occasions been invited to witness the wonderful physical manifestations of departed spirits in the presence of the Bangs children. These manifestations take place in a fully lighted room, and yet musical instruments have to be enclosed in a box or dark room, in order to enable spirits to play upon them. This family all seem to be mediumistic, but two little girls, aged respectively eleven and seven years, are considered the best mediums. The manifestations were so varied in our presence that we can give but a faint outline of them in this article. A long, heavy, extension dining table is brought out, and an ordinary table cloth is spread over it. The family are seated along one side, and as many as is convenient fill up the circle around the table, excepting a space of about three feet between two of the children, which is left vacant. In this vacancy is placed a chair. The audience who may be present are seated around the room. It is then quite usual for someone in the family to ask a little spirit-son of the Bangs parents if all is right. This little son passed to spirit-life when only fourteen months old, but is now plainly seen and talked with by the other children. In response to that inquiry, an affirmative or negative answer is given by a certain number of raps or tips of the table, or by the tipping of the vacant chair above referred to. If the answer be in the negative, one of the children puts a slate under the table, upon which a pencil is laid. Immediately the sound of writing is heard on the slate, and yet the hand of the child and the slate where she holds it is in plain sight. As soon as the sound of writing ceases, the slate is placed on the table, and thereon is found, in plain English, such corrections as are required to be made in the circle to improve conditions for better manifestations. Sometimes, someone plays the piano; then the chair above referred to, dances (apparently with delight) keeping time to the music without anything or anyone touching it. The table, also, often hops and skips about like an intelligent being, keeping time with delight to the music.

---

one of the most famous propagandist of Spiritualism, unequalled in her zeal and enthusiasm. Two of her most important works were *Modern American Spiritualism*, 1870, and *Nineteenth Century Miracles*, 1884.

The children are also *clairaudient*. They hear the spirits talk, and give what they say to members of the séance, whereupon the spirits in return give their assent to the truth thereof by raps on the table, or by forcibly tipping the vacant chair. This chair seems to answer a very important purpose. It is always ready to respond to anyone's inquiries when requested. For instance, one directing an inquiry to the chair says: "Chair, is John Smith (or some less noted character), present?" The chair immediately responds by one, two, or three emphatic tips, which are understood to mean respectively, no—I don't know—yes. One wants to have a spirit friend write something on the slate, whereupon one of the little girls holds the slate under the table as before described, or on top of her head. Immediately the pencil is heard writing, and as soon as the sound ceases, she takes down the slate, and the inquirer finds a short message to him or her, and sometimes, as is claimed, in the facsimile handwriting of the deceased person while in this life. In all these cases, as hundreds of skeptics can testify, the writing is done without the touch of any mortal hand.

A little box is fitted up, and a number of musical instruments are placed in the same. One of the little girls will sit by the side of the box, with one hand inserted through a little hole, only to the wrist joint, all in plain sight of the audience. Then the musical instruments will be played, several at a time, keeping time with a piano played in the room. Dancing will also be heard, etc. Hands are often presented at a little diamond shaped hole in the box, moving things which have been deposited in the box. The last manifestations are the most perfect when a little seven year old girl is tied fast and placed inside of the box.

Another most interesting phase is also witnessed. While you are looking right at one of these little girls, you will hear her cry out, "Oh!" in a child-like voice, as if she were hurt. She will push up her sleeve, and there will be found in plain and deep indentations in the muscle of the arm, a set of children's teeth—upper and lower—indeed, in some instances, almost drawing blood. She will slip down her sleeve, and no sooner down than she cries out again as before, and again slips up her sleeve, and other indentations similar to the first are seen, and this will be repeated for a half dozen times or more, while you are looking right at her all the time. She says it feels exactly as if she was being bit by a child, and, indeed, the arm presents that appearance.

Emma Hardinge Britten:

We might go on and recite the varied manifestations which are daily astonishing the beholders, in the presence of these children, would space admit it. We will content ourselves, for the present, by giving the following narrative, written for this paper by Mrs. Bangs, the mother of the children, under the approval of Mr. Bangs, their father:

Meroe Bangs:

I will commence by saying that up to September 30th, 1874, none of our family had ever seen any spirit manifestations, and were not thinking about them. All at once, on September 30th, about five o'clock in the evening, hard coal was thrown in at the door. I thought it to be the neighbor's children, and requested them to stop. They answered that they had not thrown any coal; but of course I did not believe them, and closed the door.

The kitchen window was dropped about six inches at the top and, after I closed the door, coal commenced to come in at the top of the window. When my husband, Mr. Bangs, came home to supper, about seven o'clock in the evening, I told him the children had been throwing coal into the house. While he was at supper the coal kept coming in all the time. After supper Mr. Bangs went out around the house and concealed himself, with the expectation that he could find out who it was that threw the coal, but failed to see anyone, but he could see the coal pass in at the window, and hear it fall on the floor. It was a pleasant evening, and the moon shone very bright. If there had been anyone nearby he would have seen them. Mr. Bangs then came into the house and shut the window. Several pieces fell into the room after that. The next morning, about seven o'clock, coal commenced to come in at the pantry window on the other side of the house, and next it came into the dining room. From seven to eleven o'clock nearly a peck was thrown in. We were not disturbed during meal hours, nor after eight o'clock in the evening. Coal continued to come in for four days. It made no difference whether the windows or doors were open or not. One large piece was dropped in the front room, weighing eight to ten pounds, when all the doors and windows were closed. Several other large pieces were brought in and scattered in different places. Several of the neighbors were called in and can testify to the truth of this statement. They said it was some evil spirit that had got into the house.

The next day, chairs and other articles of furniture were piled up together in plain view in a moment, and then returned to their places again. Dishes were put on the children's heads. A brick, and a tumbler full of water, was placed on the head of one of the girls several times. Nearly every dish and small article in the house was put on their heads, and kept me busy all day taking them off.

When evening came, they took the ribbon off the eldest girl's head, and tied her fast to the chair with it, and did many other things. They tipped the chair she was sitting in. I had the impression to give her a piece of paper and pencil, and I asked the question, who it was making those demonstrations. Immediately they controlled one of the girl's hands, and wrote, 'good spirit', the girl not having any control of her hands. In a day or two after that, she saw the spirit of Mrs. Bangs' sister, and described her form and features perfectly. She never saw her in life. The spirit spoke in an audible voice several times, calling Mr. Bangs, "Brother Edward! Brother Edward!" One time when the children were not in the house, at another time when the children were asleep in bed.

The lamp was trimmed every day, for two weeks, by spirit hands, the wick being cut each time. Dishes were washed, knives were scoured by them in a few moments, and beds were made. The pantry floor was washed, and another floor was swept. One day, while the eldest girl, Elizabeth, was ironing one part of a garment, a spirit took another iron and ironed the other part and helped until all the clothes were ironed. I saw the iron move about on the cloth, but could not see the spirit. Presents were brought for the girls, and carried into the school-room and given to them. They had each a new circular comb and neck ribbon given to them in the school-house. The combs were put into their hair and the ribbons tied around their necks. They did not know anything about it till some of the scholars asked them where they got their new combs and ribbons.

The spirit who wrote through our daughter, Elizabeth's hand, said that she wanted our family to hold a circle every evening for development. We did so. The first evening, they tipped the table, and telegraphed by raps, our daughter hearing the voice of the spirit and, at the same time giving directions what they wanted us to do next. We sang, and they kept time to the music, by raps and dancing on the floor. We heard the sound of their feet plainly. That evening the children saw other spirits of our departed friends. Among them was our little boy, who passed away when only fourteen months old. Since that time he seems to be constantly with us. He has drawn pictures on paper and on the slate, and writes on the slate without the aid of natural hands, giving very intelligent communications. One evening, while all the family were sitting at the supper table, with a full light, our little girl Mary had her dress changed in a few moments by spirit power. We are all positive she did not move from her chair during the meal, and yet her dress was changed, and the dress they took off from her was carried and hung up, in her room. Quite often, the girls have had their dresses thus changed, and their hair curled before our eyes, that is, we could see that their clothes were changed, and their hair curled, but could not see any one doing it, but we know the girls did not do it. The spirits have bought toys and other useful articles, and brought them into the house. They use their own money. Several times they have given the children small pieces of silver money and currency. I said to the spirits one day that I wished them to put a piece of money on the girl's head if they could. I kept looking at her all the time. In a few moments they put twenty five cents on her head. I know she did not have any money about her, and could not have put it there while I was watching. One day I put an apron in a bureau drawer, and locked the drawer. In a few moments the same article was thrown out from a little box or cabinet in another part of the sitting room. I put it back in the bureau drawer, and locked it in the drawer three times in succession, with the same result. The spirits have written many times on a slate placed on the girl's head, without using any visible pencil, or anything but their own hands. Some of the best communications we have had, have been written on the slate, as it lay on the head of the medium. There are many other manifestations of a startling nature which I will omit to mention.

This article being already longer than I thought it would be when I commenced it, in conclusion, I will say that we have a large band of spirits with us all the time—some of them our near relations who seem ever ready to manifest their presence. They say all our family are mediums. I will give the names and ages of the children. Elizabeth is eleven; Mary is eight; William is six; and Edward is fourteen years of age.

Chicago, March 10th, Mrs. M. L. Bangs

Emma Hardinge Britten:

The author would scarcely have ventured to print a narrative so full of *incredible commonplaces*, were it not that several persons of undoubted credit have testified to being present in Mrs. Bangs house when invisible servitors laid the dinner table, and brought in one after another the articles necessary for the meals, whilst the witnesses sat by and watched the proceedings in the full light of day.

As in many other instances on record, a large number of residents of Chicago who have visited this wonderful family, as mere acquaintances, affirm that the spontaneous demonstrations, occurring in the routine of private family life, are far more wonderful than any which can be obtained in circles, or through processes of invocation. This is a phase of phenomenal power testified to by all who have had the privilege of visiting mediumistic persons in their own house.

CHAPTER *2*

INDEPENDENT SLATE WRITING

─────────►●◄─────────

"Human experience, which is constantly contradicting theory, is the great test of truth"

~ SAMUEL JOHNSON

There would be no exaggeration in saying that Elizabeth and May Bangs, during their heyday, were two of the finest mediums in the world for independent writing, done above-board and in full light. Slates were used, usually the early hinged type or simply two single slates, and when closed up or placed together, one on top the other, it created in between them, a tiny "cabinet" or darkened area for the spirit operators to use. Rarely were both sisters needed for this phenomenon unless extra power was required. Sitters could bring their own slates and blank sheets of paper; these would be put into an envelope or simply folded and put between the slates and in ways inscrutable to mortal man—as are all spiritual phenomena until he enters the world of spirit himself—words would be precipitated on to the blank pages of paper, usually in ink, a small bottle of which would be placed on top of the slates, which were tightly bound by heavy rubber bands or cords by the sitter. The sitter in most cases would have written previous to the sitting, and without the mediums ever seeing them, a series of questions on the pages of paper and then include blank pages for the spirit of whom they wished to communicate with to answer them. In other instances the spirit writing would be done directly on to the enclosed slates. Another name for this phenomenon within Spiritualism, was Psychography or Direct Writing.[7]

Spirit Writing by spirit John Gray

Now, the writing is not produced either by personal contact of the medium or his spirit friends. Everything done in the spirit world is done by natural law, and it would be an unnatural law that would permit a materialized hand to go between the surface of slates one-sixteenth of an inch apart and grasp a pencil to write. The principal methods we use to transmit messages are by the law that is beginning to be well known and understood by you mortals on earth, by electricity and magnetism. We also have other methods of producing the writing, etc. One of them is by transference; that is to say we can prepare sufficient writing or pictures in the spirit world to fill the surface of the medium's slate, and then transfer it instantaneously upon said slate. To produce this manifestation we must first thoroughly sensitize the slate to be operated upon, and disintegrate the pencil into fine powder and precipitate it evenly over the surface of the slate. The transfer is made somewhat similar to photography. The color writing is produced through somewhat the same method, except that the color matter is procured on your earth plane and brought into the room and on the slates the same as the former. The latter methods are much more difficult to produce, and better conditions are required. It is also indispensable to have the medium in a healthy state, free from all the mundane worry and annoyance, with pleasant surroundings, and everything that is possible to make him happy, harmonious, and contented. This is important, and good mediums for this phase should not be overworked, but should be carefully protected by those who value the evidence obtained through their mediumship.

---

[7] See *Psychography* by M.A.Oxon (William Stainton Moses), London, 1882; *Psychography* by J. J. Owen, 1897; *Twixt Two Worlds*, by J. S. Farmer, London, 1886; *Slate Writing-Invisible Intelligence*, by Ron Nagy, 2009; *Startling Facts in Modern Spiritualism*, by N. B. Wolfe, 1875; *Transcendental Physics*, by Zollner, 1880.

As a parting word to investigators, I would recommend that they approach the medium for investigation in a pleasant, harmonious manner, with their eyes wide open if in doubt, and they will win the medium's sympathy, and thus make conditions which will insure good results instead of in the case with many who, with loud voices, while admitting they have never sat with a medium, proclaim their belief that the manifestation they expect to receive will be fraudulent. I suppose it is human nature for all to rebel at insults and aspersions against their honesty, and especially is it the case when the attack is made by parties who admit that you have never given them cause for these cruel charges. A medium being more sensitive that the ordinary run of mortals, feels these insults more than they, and the result is that the possibility of a satisfactory séance is spoiled by the rebellious state of the medium.

Yours in aid to a knowledge of a future life.

~ John Gray

That spirits should be able to write or sketch in the restricted space between two slates, under observation in daylight, seems a marvelous phenomenon; and when writing is done on a sheet of paper placed between the pages of a closed book, the marvel seems even greater. But even these phenomena seem to be eclipsed in wonder by those which occurred in the presence of the two young mediums, the Misses Lizzie and May Bangs, of Chicago, U. S. A., and which were witnessed by hundreds of people, including many reliable psychical researchers....the phenomena were truly astounding.

~ A. Campbell Holmes

We had two important experiments in December, 1909 (with the conjurer Mr. William Marriott), to ascertain if he could copy the Bangs' manifestations without his methods (admittedly conjuring) being detected. Both were clever and amusing attempts, but unsuccessful.

~ Admiral W. Usborne Moore

"We cannot but speak the things we have seen and heard."

~ *ACTS 4:20*

TESTIMONIES

May Wright Sewell (1844-1920),[8] American educator, reformer and lecturer, holder of bachelor and master's degrees, best known for her work with the woman's Suffrage movement and with women's organizations worldwide. Among numerous other achievements, she was appointed by President McKinley, in 1899, to represent the women of the United States at a series of congresses for *l' Exposition Universelle* at Paris in 1900. The medium is referred to in a footnote in her book as only 'Miss Bangs, of Chicago, and "Miss B." Mrs. Sewell sought communication with her late husband.

Mrs. Sewell:

Mr. G. gave me a note of introduction to a lady of whom I had never heard, saying that he felt himself moved to give it in the same way that he had felt moved to seek my acquaintance, and that while he had received nothing from any source that one would call a communication and nothing but his "feelings" to reply upon, he believed this introduction was "impulse" and would lead to a significant experience.

The second day after my arrival I separated myself from my friend and, presenting the letter of introduction furnished by Mr. G., arranged for a professional interview with its recipient at four thirty p.m. the next day. When our hour arrived rain was falling heavily and the wind was violent. Miss B. said that the conditions were unfavorable. To my inquiry how the storm could affect the conditions, her reply was that she did not know *how*, but that as fact "the electrical conditions of the atmosphere do modify the vibrations, and they say everything depends on vibrations." In assertions of fact, Miss B. was as positive as other psychics I had questioned, apparently more vague in explanation, and even more ignorant of the causes of phenomena. She said she had always from her childhood "been accompanied by phenomena,"

---

[8]   *Neither Dead Nor Sleeping*, M.W. Sewell, London, Watkins, 1921

but never thought about cause; it did not interest her. I gained no new knowledge of principles, but I added two new facts to my accumulation of material for reflection. For the first time I received "independent writing on paper," and also carried on a long coherent, satisfactory conversation by means of a " private telegraphic code." As this was my first experience of them I shall describe both processes.

Miss B. and myself sat on opposite sides of a small table which, with our two chairs, a carpet, a few framed photographs on the wall, and a few trifles on the mantel above a small fireplace, constituted the sole furniture of a small back parlor. I think its dimensions were not more than eight by ten. On top of the table were two slates and a bottle of ink.

As the process mentioned last was the first employed I will describe it first. I propounded questions to my husband exactly as if he had been present in the flesh and his replies were made as if by telegraph; the tick, tick, tick coming to the ear exactly as if clicked on the machine at a telegraphic office, was read by Miss B. just as an arriving telegram would be read by a telegraph operator. The answers and comments, like my questions, pertained to subjects, persons, places and events which in the nature of things must have been utterly unknown to the operator; but there was not an instant's hesitation nor was there a irrelevant word; and, as events proved, where the conduct of persons in relation to matters not yet matured was involved, there was not one mistaken opinion uttered.

I next wrote a letter containing numerous questions, folded it with several sheets of blank paper and sealed it in an envelope addressed to my husband. Having washed off two slates, I placed the sealed letter between them, tied them fast with my own handkerchief, and held them firmly in my hands. Miss B. then dropped some ordinary black ink on a small bit of ordinary blotting paper, and placed it on the upper surface of the top slate, I holding the slates firmly all the time, and I alone touching them. In a few moments Miss B. said that my letter was answered. I thereupon untied the slates and on opening the envelope found that the paper which I had put in *blank* was covered with clear script in black ink in a writing resembling but not duplicating that of my husband. There were six pages, which when read proved to be an orderly, coherent, categorical reply to my letter. The *answers* were numbered to correspond with numbered questions.

I was too astonished to have any wish but to withdraw to reread this novel communication.

As I expressed this feeling and rose to go, the click of telegraphy began and Miss B., interpreting it, said: "Your husband wishes to know if you have some other desire." I replied that I was always wishing for the long-ago promised portrait of himself and wished that in some way he could contrive to give it to me for our anniversary, or at least for my next Christmas gift.

In Chapter 3, the full report of Mrs. Sewell's spirit portrait sitting will be included. It is obvious that she, with senses intact and on the alert, controlled the conditions of the slate sitting with "Miss B." from start to finish. It also seems that the communicating spirit uses an amanuensis, a literary assistant who takes dictation, and this seems plausible within the fact that the actual handwriting in the Bangs slate communications, in many instances, seems the same.

S. J. Gibson, of Meadville, PA.

His account while visiting Lily Dale, reported by the *Tribune-Republican* and published in *The Sunflower,* September 1st, 1901:

I thought perhaps the readers of the *Tribune- Republican* would like to hear from this beautiful camp, Lily Dale, and some of the phenomena of which I have been an eyewitness. The first I will relate is a message, or communication, which was given to Judge C. D. Clark of Willoughby, O. Judge Clark had in his possession a pair of slates that had been riveted together before he left home.

After he arrived at this camp he prepared a letter at the hotel where he was stopping. He took six sheets of tablet paper, which had the hotel address on, and wrote on one sheet the name of the departed son he wished to hear from, and put them in one of the hotel envelopes, sealed the envelopes, took the envelope and slates to the Bangs Sisters' cottage and engaged a daylight sitting.

He had his riveted slates with him, which he was told to place on the table, and to put his sealed envelopes between two of the Bangs Sisters slates, which were lying on the table. By further direction he placed rubber bands around the slates, which contained the envelope, then placed those slates on top of his riveted slates and held his hands on them.

One of the mediums held her hands on the slates a portion of the time, when ready for the demonstration, and in a short time raps were heard on the slates, in which he had placed his sealed letter, and found it gone. The mediums told him he would find the envelope enclosed between the riveted slates. The judge took the riveted slates to the office of the association, procured a file and opened the slates in the presence of 100 people, I being an eyewitness to the operation. When the riveted slates were opened the judge's sealed envelope was found between them, and the seal was unbroken. He opened the letter in our presence, and the papers were found written full, some on both sides and done in ink. The communication was from his son. The entire demonstration was done in the full light of day.

I wonder where "Mr. Critic" could go with the obvious dematerialization of the letter from the slates on top with Mr. Gibson's hands on top of them, to the riveted slates below and the unbroken seal on the envelope afterwards?

The next little section deals with the rarest of the rare reports on the astonishing demonstrations by Lizzie Bangs of spirit typewriting.

Independent Typewriting
The Progressive Thinker
Chicago
November 21st, 1891
Manifestations at Muncie, Indiana

To the Editor

Miss Lizzie S. Bangs, of your city, by special arrangement and agreement was induced to come here for one week, for the purpose of giving private sittings for independent slate writing. While here she gave thirty or more sittings—all of which were perfectly satisfactory. Some had the slates placed on the floor, or hung on the gas fixture in the center of the room.

Miss Bangs was so well received and pleased that she promised to come again.

Light: Journal of Psychical, Occult and Mystical Research
Quaestor Vitae
Saturday, December 7th, 1895

Professor Aimes made an interesting statement on Sunday, November 3rd, on the platform of Carnegie Hall, with regard to an experience of typewriting without human contact, which occurred in Chicago during the World's Fair, in the presence of another medium, Mrs. Bangs. He sat with the medium and three other people, who, joining hands, formed a circle round the machine, in the dark. He himself sat opposite and in front of the keys, the medium sitting at one side. When the keys began to operate, without leaving go of the hands of his neighbors he bent his head down over the machine till his face almost touched the keys, the keys continuing to work. There was not room, he says, for a hand, spirit or human, to intervene between his face and the keys. This would apparently infer that the keys were not worked by a materialized hand, as some suppose, but rather by transference of energy. When the first message was finished, the sheet was taken out and put into a box beneath the machine and a fresh sheet of paper adjusted into the machine, by the invisible powers. Five messages were thus written and put into this 'post box,' when the séance was declared to have terminated, and a message for each sitter was found to have been written and addressed, one to each person present. Professor Aimes stated that he himself employs three typewriters, but the writing thus effected in total darkness, while his head was almost in contact with the keys, was more rapid than could be done by any of his secretaries.

Light of Truth
Vol.12
Cincinnati
Saturday, June 17th, 1893

"A New Mode of Spirit Communication:
Communications Through the Typewriter"
By George Lieberknecht

On Wednesday night, May 10th, I was one of a small circle for witnessing manifestations at the residence of Miss Lizzie Bangs, 10 South Elizabeth Street, Chicago. The Bangs are well known as remarkable mediums for independent slate writing and other phenomena. The circle consisted on six men and one lady besides the medium. The sitters were mostly, if not entirely strangers to one another. We were seated closely and compactly around a small table with hands joined. On the small table in the center was placed a typewriter. Before the lights were put out the door was locked. The medium occupied a place in the circle just like the rest of us but facing the back not the front of the typewriter. This is a recent development in Miss Bangs mediumship and is one more striking evidence of the progress of the invisible operations on the other side are making in bringing the gulf between us and them, and in perfecting and multiplying the avenues of intelligent and rapid communication.

I feel confident in saying the medium does not touch the typewriter at all; it is used independent of or without contact from the medium's hands or fingers. There is no holding or hesitating in the action of the machine; on the contrary, you hear that it is operated with an astonishing degree of swiftness and dexterity. When one letter or message is finished, the sheet is removed, folded up, addressed on the machine, and then the next one printed, until each one of the company has one. The one addressed to the writer of this article from his son contains one hundred and eighty-six words. In mechanical execution this independent typewriting, of which I examined several specimens at the close of the séance, is done in a neat, clear business-like manner, and although a punctilious critic could point out some errors in punctuation, etc., the performance is as good as the letters one receives from first class business houses.

Let any expert type writer try to write under the same conditions, and compare the results. For me, it was a manifestation which impressed me more deeply than all the din and uproar, all the show and ostentation of the big city.

Spiritualism brings the knowledge which satisfies and lifts above the material world, which means from sordid selfishness and narrowness of spirit, and makes this world and the present life a foot-stool for larger growth and the unfolding of a spiritual humanity.

GENESEO, ILLINOIS MAY, 1893

Mr. A. B. Richmond

Attorney, Meadville, PA., medical degree from Allegheny College, author of *The Seybert Commission Report Addendum*, 1888.[9]
Lily Dale, New York

After having visited another medium at Lily Dale, Mr. Richmond reported: "The day after experiment No.2, August 7, 1888, I procured two clean slates and visited Miss Lizzie Bangs. I prepared an interrogatory and placed it with a fragment of pencil between the slates, tied a string around them, and laid them on a table placed in the center of a well-lighted room, the window and door being open. The medium was seated opposite me, the slates between us on the table; they were not out of my sight one moment. I placed my hand on one end of the slates, Miss Bangs placing hers on the other end. We sat thus and conversed for some time, I relating to her my experience with Mr. Rowley in Cleveland. Soon I heard a faint noise between the slates. It did not sound like writing, but more like the crawling of an insect imprisoned between them; in a few moments there came three distinct raps. I opened the slates and found two messages written in the Morse alphabet, one of them signed by the one to whom the interrogatory was directed, and could not in this life read or write telegraphy; the other was by a prominent jurist who died a number of years ago. I made an appointment for another séance the next day, and procured two new clean slates, I passed a screw through each end of the frames. At the appointed time I again visited Miss Lizzie Bangs. I opened the slates and permitted her to place a small piece of pencil between them; then closing them I screwed them securely together. I told the medium I desired that she should not touch the slates, and therefore I placed

---

9   See *Spirit Writing*, Ron Nagy 2009; *Encyclopedia of Psychic Science*, Nandor Fodor, 1966.

them under the tablecloth, yet holding them with my hands, firmly clasping their sides. Miss Bangs laid her fingers lightly on the ends of the slates, outside of the cloth. Very soon I heard a pencil write; in a moment it ceased, and the medium picked up a slate of her own and wrote very rapidly the following: "Have partially written a message, will finish it another time - George." I did not open the slates, but took them to my hotel room and locked them in my trunk. The next day I again visited the medium, placed the slates under the tablecloth, holding them as before. Soon I heard a slight "ticking" sound beneath the cloth, and soon it ceased, and Miss Bangs wrote on her slate the following:

"Have done much toward finishing the message, but will have to have one more sitting, the forces not being sufficient to conclude it. Do not open the slates, for we will surely give you that for which you are seeking and desire. Yours, George H. S."

Again I took the slates to my hotel and locked them in my trunk. The next day I visited the medium and placed the slates as before. I waited patiently over half an hour, heard no sound, when Miss Bangs again wrote on her slate: "We cannot write on the slates today, but will another time." I have said that the medium "wrote on her slate," I mean by that, that she placed the slate on her lap, under the table, holding it with one hand, while the other remained on the cloth over the slates on top of the table; and although I watched her arm, as closely as you state that you did the thumb of the medium, on page 21 of your admirable report, yet I did not see the least movement. (He was filing a report as an addendum to the *Seybert Commission Report*, an impotent, cowardly report by old, highly titled men, in March 1884, most of whom—with the exception of Thomas R. Hazard, the only Spiritualist on the committee—were prejudiced against Spiritualism and Mediumship. In 1887 this committee published a preliminary report with negative conclusions in the entire field of spiritualistic phenomena. No final report was ever published, nor was the investigation ever continued or resumed – Ed.).

You will observe gentleman, that I pursued your astute method of investigation; I observed what was going on above the table without regard to the mysterious phenomena transpiring beneath it. In fact, I did not care who wrote beneath the table; I was only determined that there should be no fraud practiced on my slates, which were securely fastened together with screws, as narrated, and held by me alone, on top of the table.

The next day I again visited the medium, and placed the slates as before. We sat nearly an hour. I became impatient, but remembering the terrible ordeal your chairman endured in his effort to become a medium, I imitated his Job like patience, and continued the séance until I became satisfied that no result would be obtained that day, and made another appointment. The next day I visited the medium, placed the slates as before. Each time I had carefully held them with the screw heads upward, and from the "slots" in the heads of the screws I had drawn a pencil mark on the frames, so that if the screws were turned without my knowledge I would observe it with a magnifying-glass, even if I could not see it with the naked eye.

As soon as the medium placed her fingers over the end of the slates, I heard the pencil write most vigorously, and so loudly that it could have been heard across the room. When the writing ceased, I opened the slates and was surprised to find on the lower slate a communication in Latin, and one in telegraphy, while the upper slate was filled with a communication signed by Henry Seybert.[10] I will have these slates photographed, and you will doubtless observe the fact that the handwriting is the same as that on the slate observed by me over a year ago through Mr. Keeler, a photograph of which I sent to you at this time.

I can only wonder where those historic slates could be? Mr. Richmond's indefatigable efforts seemed to pay off. He brought some life to the original banal, humdrum published by the Seybert Commission.

I know of no one in Great Britain in whose powers of observation I could place greater reliance than those of Admiral Moore. This distinguished naval officer occupied several important positions, and served the Government of his country in command of warships specially fitted out for scientific research—which need not be detailed here—all of which redounded to his credit, and received his country's thanks.

~ JAMES COATES, PH. D., 1911

---

[10] Henry Seybert, a Philadelphia Spiritualist, and the very man who had left $60,000 in his will to the University of Pennsylvania for the express purpose of making an exhaustive, scientific investigation of Spiritualism.

VICE ADMIRAL W. USBORNE MOORE (1850-1918)

Admiral Moore, when he retired as a Commander in the British Navy, dedicated his life to psychical research and, in my opinion became what I consider, a champion for the cause of truth by reporting in a non-prejudicial, pragmatic manner what he himself witnessed. His seminal works, *Glimpses of the Next State*, 1911, (one of the greatest books of Spiritualism) and The Voices, 1913[11] now, wonderfully republished by White Crow Books, are a study in physical mediumship. *The Voices* only blessed even more the field of psychical research by continuing his documentation of one of the finest Direct Voice mediums of the 20th century, Etta Wriedt, about whom he had originally written in *Glimpses*.

Since this is a complete work, involving and including as much relevant and available material as I could find involving the Bangs Sisters, it is an honor and privilege to include the work of Admiral Moore, who did more to certify the legitimacy and genuineness of the Bangs' mediumship than any other individual. There was a brief, but aggressively publicized controversy involving Moore and another well-known British researcher, Hereward Carrington, and this is dealt with later on.

The Bangs Sisters at Chicago
Admiral W. Usborne Moore

One of the principal reasons for my visiting the United States was to see the phenomena described to me in the following letter, dated October 19, 1908, by a gentleman of considerable position and influence in Canada.

Our next experience was at Chicago, with the Bangs Sisters, of whom we had heard both good and evil reports. We were, in consequence, especially alert. I will leave you to judge of what we obtained there. We were told by friends who had visited them to write our questions before going to the house, and place them, with a number of blank sheets of stamped initialled paper, inside an envelope gummed and sealed. This we did, using paper from a Toledo hotel that was decorated with a gilt monogram. We reached Chicago early on the following morning.

---

[11] *Glimpses of the Next State*, 1911, *The Voices*, Vice-Admiral W. Usborne Moore, 1913, London: Watts & Co., White Crow Books, 2012.

At nine o'clock we had found the Bangs residence and secured an immediate séance, before the arrival of their numerous clients. We sat with Miss May Bangs. To this day she is ignorant of our names or where we came from; nor had she any inkling of our visit or its purpose. We accompanied her, each in turn, into a comfortable little boudoir on the sunny side of the house looking out on a bit of lawn; the only window remained open. In the center of the room was a table, four feet square, covered with a woollen cloth. The medium sat opposite to me, about a foot or more from the table; the only object on the table was an open inkstand. I said I had brought with me some questions in a sealed envelope, and hoped to obtain replies through her mediumship. She said, "We will try." She then fetched a pair of hinged slates, the frames of which were covered with dark cloth, gave them to me, and resumed her seat, saying, "Place your letter between the slates, close them, and secure them with these stout rubber bands; lay the slates on the table, in front of you, and place both hands flat on top of them."

The medium's instructions having been carried out, we engaged in general conversation. Three times she interrupted the talk to ask, "Is this name or place correctly spelt?"

(Foreign names mentioned in my questions), showing that some knowledge of what I had written was reaching her. If I assented, or made a slight correction, she would write on a pad resting on her knee; then resumed our conversation where it had dropped.

About half-an-hour was thus spent, when three distinct raps were heard and felt by me, proceeding, apparently, from the center of the table. Miss Bangs then said: "The séance is over; you have obtained what you are to get; you may open your envelope now or later." I opened the hinged slates, found the envelope as I had placed it, untouched and still sealed, thanked the lady, and left the room, when my brother passed in for his turn.

While waiting for my brother, in the adjoining room, I slit open the end of my envelope with my penknife, and found, besides my questions, nine and a half pages of the blank paper covered with writing in ink, as if with a steel pen, duly numbered, and written as the instance of the spirit friend to whom I had addressed four out of five questions, and signed in full. The replies were categorical, giving or confirming information of great value to me personally; referring to facts and happenings of forty years ago, which the spirit and I alone were aware of; and adding the names of individuals whom I had not named in my questions, but whom we both knew in the past, and who had participated in the events referred to by me.

The reply to the fifth and last question was in the form of greetings from spirit friends who were known to me when they were in earth life, and now come to me as so-called

"Guides."

When one writes rapidly, a blotter is necessary at the turnover to a new page; this, apparently, was not required by the spirit writer, for the ink was in the same depth of black at the foot as the top of the pages. The handwriting of the last message (and each signature at the bottom of it) differs from that which contained replies to my first four questions.

It is not claimed that this writing is done by spirit friends themselves, but, at their dictation, by the medium's control, who has become expert in this form of manifestation.

Can telepathy account for these replies? Can it explain the transfer of the ink from the bottle on the table to the folded blank pages within the sealed envelope between the slates under my hands? It would take a very fast writer at least an hour and a quarter to write what the spirit performed in half an hour, and this is leaving out of consideration the deliberation required for penning the involved replies to my questions. I regret that they are of such a personal nature that I cannot even send you extracts.

My brother's replies covered about thirteen pages; among them were three signed notes from three different spirit friends who had come to him in my house, or at Detroit, at the Jonsons', in Toledo."

(MATERIALIZATION MEDIUM, EXTRAORDINAIRE, J. B. JONSON)

Admiral Moore:

On the way up from New York I had heard a great deal of evil about the Bangs Sisters; and I had also seen five of the pictures done, as their owners told me, in their presence, within three feet of them, by invisible agency, and through the mediumship of these women, whose only participation in the production was that they held the canvases. I wished to make a thorough test of both letters and pictures. Many people in London were much interested in the Canadian gentleman's account. It had been the theme and discussion, and I was determined not to return to England without making the best attempt I could to solve the mystery.

January 17, 1909

I arrived in Chicago and called upon the Bangs Sisters by appointment at 6 p.m., ostensibly for arranging sittings for the week. I persuaded May Bangs, however, to sit with me that evening for a letter. In anticipation of her consent, I had brought one in my pocket. She showed me into a small room some 12 ft. by 8 ft., and produced two slates, between which I placed my letter. We sat at a small oak table, which measured 3 ft. 8 in. by 2 ft. 4 in., covered with a green cloth that did not extend anywhere beyond the top. May Bangs pinched one end of the two slates together while I secured them with four rubber bands, two one way and two the other. My letter was written to my guide, Iola, and inside the envelope I had enclosed four blank sheets of blank Secor Hotel (Toledo) paper for the expected reply. This paper was all marked with a private mark; the envelope was closed with a two-cent postage stamp.

Upon the slates, now in my hands, she put a small pot of ink, and over that a piece of Bristol-board very slightly larger than the slates. She then said, (as if impressed with some doubt): "Have you addressed this spirit, to whom you are writing, by a definite name?" "No," I replied. "Then please write the name on a piece of paper and put it on top of the slates." This I did without her being able to see what I was writing; the paper was doubled and placed my side of the pot of ink under the Bristol-board. Now she began to see clairvoyantly, and described the form of a young lady whom I recognized as Iola, bringing two old people whom I gathered from her talk to be my father and mother. She also saw two young men (probably my brothers in spirit life).

She now began, sentence by sentence, to give me the exact questions in my letter. Presently she said: "Is this the name?" and handed me, from the pad she held, a piece of paper upon which was written quite plainly the Christian and surname of Iola when in earth life, the same name I had written on the piece of paper now on the slates close under my hand. She also said: "Your paper with the name has gone in between the slates."

All this time May Bangs was sitting one foot away from the table on the opposite side to me, with a writing-pad and pencil in her hands, which were two feet from the slates. The gas was burning brightly.

Three-quarters of an hour had passed from the time of our sitting down, when three taps on the slates announced that the reply was finished. I took off the Bristol-board and found my pieces of paper *inside* by the letter. The latter was slit open from the top, and four pages of reply were found inside. I examined it, and found that it was the same paper I had put in at the Toledo hotel with my private mark on it.

The letter of reply contained private messages, which I am unable to make public. It was signed correctly, and answered nearly all my questions.

During the sitting May Bangs saw the form of some Eastern queen surrounded by attendants. It was obviously Cleopatra, who came to redeem her promise given the day before at Toledo.

(See List of Illustrations for Iola and Cleopatra portraits)

January 19, 1909 - 10 to 12 (noon)

Atmospheric conditions good. I took to the Bangs Sisters a letter containing two sheets (four pages) of questions. In the envelope I put four blank sheets of hotel paper marked with a private mark. The envelope which contained these six sheets was gummed and sealed with my signet ring. I had written twenty-three questions to my guide. I was received by May Bangs in the same small room, and, as before, the room was flooded with light. I put the letter between her two slates, which are covered with wool at the edges so as to exclude the faintest ray of light. She took hold of the double slate ends with one hand while I put four rubber bands round the slates, as I had done two days previously. The slates were then put on the table, the same little vessel of ink was placed on top, and over all the Bristol-board before mentioned. From this moment May Bangs had nothing to do with the slates; they were in my own possession under my hands. The psychic and I sat opposite to one another, she, leaning back in her chair, writing on a pad of paper.

After we had been sitting, talking, for a quarter of an hour, May Bangs began telling me what my questions were, and answering some of them. Presently she said, "Tear off one corner of your visiting cards, so that you can identify it again; put it on the slates, and we will see what happens to it." About fifteen minutes later she said: "Why do you write to your relative in such a formal style? Write a postscript on a piece of paper, naming your wife in the same familiar way as you would if writing to this spirit in life." This I did without her seeing what I had written, and put the piece of paper, doubled up, also on the slates. She then went on as before, repeating my questions within the sealed envelope. At 11:10 the psychic said: "Your card has gone into the letter." When an hour and three-quarters had elapsed from the time we began the sitting, three knocks on the table announced that the writing was finished.

I now opened the slates. Inside I found my packet intact, with seal untouched. On the outside of the envelope was written: "The little slip" (my postscript) "has been arranged to your hat in the other room." This was signed by an initial - the Christian name of my guide. I slit open the envelope at the top, and found inside it: (a) My questions, contained in four pages. (b) Eight pages of reply from the spirit, in ink, as if written with a steel pen. (c) My visiting card. I then went into the drawing room, where I had left my hat, found that it had been moved, and that inside the lining was my postscript.

Before I left, May Bangs read out to me the questions in my letter, which she had written on her pad as she saw them in the "astral light." They were all correct in sense, though not in actual phrasing; and the curious thing was that she read them out in precisely the proper consecutive order - (1), (2), up to (23). With some reluctance, she later eventually surrendered the pages of the pad to me; it is one of the most curious documents in my possession.

The following is the letter of reply to my questions:

My dear,

I am with you once again and, as ever, delighted to manifest my presence in ever so slight a manner. Now...you are trying me again - trying my memory of earthly things, places, and persons and how I do wish I could tear asunder the little barrier preventing me from giving free and full expression, but do you know...in all these matters my memory is perfectly clear when I stand free and unhampered in the spiritual atmosphere but somehow when I return into earth's atmosphere, so many things become hazy and incomplete; in other words, it is not designed that mortals shall know it all. If it were so, research would be of the past, and spiritual matters of earth be at a standstill. These little indifficiencies (sic) lead the mind to further inquiry, and little by little the returns bringing reassurance is given.

I am not familiar with all the laws governing spirit return in outward demonstration. I am constantly learning and in time know I shall bring the beautiful truth into your own home. I am trying and shall continue to try for the desirable conditions, for I feel coming to you, and.... alone I would find that condition of thought that heretofore has been missing, and thereby give free and full evidence of identity you so much desire. The law of evolution is carrying us onward and upward in spiritual truth just as fast as mortal mind is capable of accepting and understanding in its true light; and if at times we fail to give you all that your mind requires, do not doubt, but know, that time will reward you. It surely will, and right here I want to say to you that our beautiful "Cleopatra," who was such a wonderful intelligence here on earth, and in her many years of life and study in the higher advanced spheres in spirit life, is more capable in guiding you in these scientific problems than those who have been in spirit life in times of the past century, and to help you to solve and furnish the missing link for the world of science. This has never been given, because science in the material world has not reached an understanding of the elements and laws even of their own atmosphere. They acknowledge the existence of Electricity, its results and effect under certain conditions reached through long study and experimenting, but they cannot produce it independent in substance. It is the propelling power of all life, all action, and the time will come when your people of science will understand it better, and so there are other elements in the very atmosphere about you that spirits must understand and utilize to bring about these results. It is because of your ignorance of these elements and lack of knowledge of the average spirits, myself included, coming in contact with these laws that form the barrier of expression.

As before stated, in my own domain, all that you seek to know of me this morning is as clear as the noonday sun, but my great anxiety to have powers to give it, as also your anxiety to receive, for the time bars me in expression.

There are many subjects of your letter I would like to take in full explanation fully, but I fear I cannot in this one meeting, so I shall only refer to them briefly, for all come under the same law.

That I with you in every move you make, travelling from your own location to that of your home in England, you need not doubt. I do not take record of the intervening space of action but rush on straight, glide through space, as it were, in the twinkling of an eye. I do not know all that transpires in your daily life as to material things, but make recognition of them on the whole, and particularly of your success and happiness for this is ever uppermost in my mind.

I will go to.... and prepare her mind, so that she will overcome that timidity of spiritual matters, for I am so desirous coming to her as I have you, and believe, yes know, with her willingness and your combined efforts some wonderful demonstration may be received in the home proving this great truth.

I have been impressing the psychic power how to answer some of your inquiries, for I cannot refer to all in writing. I now feel the forces waning, and must soon close.

The little impressions forming on one of the photographs is my effort, and I hope to conclude my efforts with some manifestation conclusive and interesting to you.... Adieu.

(Signed by the earth name of Iola.)

Admiral Moore:

The handwriting is the same as that in the previous letter, and has no resemblance to that of Iola when she was in earth life. All the handwriting of replies to letters through the mediumship of the Bangs Sisters has the same characteristics, as if written or precipitated by one amanuensis. It seems probable that the spirit dictates to a "writing guide," whose idiosyncrasies creep in. There are Americanisms in the above letter which certainly did not emanate from my guide. I consider that the general tone of the letter is much in advance of the mind of the psychic in the room. The pages were numbered by the writer, and the sequence of the writing was as follows: Page 5 was found on the back of page 4, page 6 at the back of page 3, page 7 at the back of page 2.

"A Crucial and Outstanding Event"
Admiral Moore, Sir William Crookes, F. R. S.[12] &
Citrate of Lithia
January 21, 1909

Atmospheric conditions good. With May Bangs from 10.45 to 12.30.

I took with me two slates a little larger than those of the Bangs Sisters. The edges were covered with woolen stuff, as were theirs (to exclude the faintest ray of light). I also took six India-rubber bands, a five-cent bottle of ink mixed with citrate of Lithia, and a letter to an old friend, Sir A .G., who had been in spirit life some years.

I have already referred to a discussion, which took place in London before my departure, regarding the desirability of finding out if the ink used in the reply letters was the same as that in the vessel on top of the slates; it was obvious that, if this could be satisfactorily established, we should have got more than half-way to proving the supernormal character of the writing. On that occasion Sir William Crookes happened to be present, and suggested that I should mix lithium with the ink; spectroscopic investigation would enable him

---

[12] Sir William Crookes (1832-1919), one of the greatest physicists of the last century; discoverer of thallium; e-ray tube, inventor of radiometer. *Wrote Researches in The Phenomena of Modern Spiritualism*, 1898, & was republished in 1926.

to say if the two inks were, or were not, identical. Needless to remark, I adopted his kind advice, and, before starting for America, I bought a small quantity of citrate of Lithia from Messrs. Cruse and Co., Dispensing Chemists, 63 Palmerston Road, Southsea. A five-cent bottle of ink was bought at "The Fair" in Chicago, about one third of it was poured out, the whole of the citrate was poured into the bottle, and well shaken up. From this mixture a little cup was filled by myself and put on the slates; the bottle was then corked and put into my coat pocket.

The letter that I wrote to Sir A. G. was as follows:

Dear Sir A-
I had the pleasure of hearing of you at Detroit on the 9th, when we had a chat about Maine disaster. The ideas you then expressed did not coincide with your opinion while in earth life. Will you kindly identify yourself as well as possible to me, and tell me what you now know as to the loss of the Maine?

Very Sincerely Yours, W. Usborne Moore

Sir A. G. held the position of English Consul-General in Cuba during the Spanish-American War. We had held conversations in London, after he retired, on the catastrophe; and his opinion was that it was due to some want of precaution on board the ship, not to the outside explosion of a mine. At Detroit he had expressed the opposite view. The reply was as follows:

I am glad to come to you today, and thank you for the privilege you grant in this grand phenomenon, demonstrative that life is indeed eternal. There are many subjects I would love to converse with you, giving my knowledge as gained from the higher side of life; but I see you have placed before me, in your letter of today, the subject of the Maine disaster. Well, my good friend, I did come to you in a recent communication differing very much indeed in ideas of this disaster from my opinion when in earth form. When I reached life, and learned of the true life and greater possibilities, this was one of the many subjects that interested me. My sympathies and indignation was touched deeply over the matter when in the physical form, and so little of the real foundation of the disaster could be reached that

I carried the desire of proving definitely the secret with me in to the new life.

I have since looked very closely into the entire object and modus operandi, and solved the mystery; this I imparted to you in a recent conversation. Thus my change of opinion since entering the higher life, but my good friend, I have also learned that all the circumstances of earth life are for a purpose. Looking from a material standpoint, many incidents, conditions, etc., would seem very unnecessary to the rounding out of a perfect life here; yet, if all was perfectly smooth, uniform and harmonious, there would be no inquiry, that disposition or inclination to greater knowledge. And without the wrong you would not be able to judge the right. So all the mistakes, disappointments, and failures in life are a necessary lesson that we shall all understand sometime when we start as equal in the higher realms of eternal life. Mine has been a wonderful experience since passing through the great change and I find today that summing up all the problems solved, I have, only yet, just begun.

Life is indeed wonderful and the more we learn of its laws, purposes and possibilities, the greater our experiences here, and hereafter the more fully we realize that which time and eternity holds for us.

I am glad to have met you in this way, my good friend; and I shall hope to have the privilege of coming frequently in thought exchange. I shall be glad to give you further information on any subject you choose to the best of my present knowledge and experience, gathered in my new life.

YOURS AS OF EARTH, A .G.

There is a resemblance between the handwriting of this letter and the other two.

Directly we went into the room I asked May Bangs to sit on the opposite side of the table to that where she usually sat. "Change the table round?" she asked. "No" I replied, " I want your drawer my side. You take out of the drawer what you want and put it on the chair or table beside you." She said, "Very well, I will do so." She simply asked to see the letter, and she held my slates while I put round them four rubber bands, two one way, two the other. I then poured my own ink into the little vessel, which holds about a teaspoon and three quarters. The card was put over all. We held the card and slates together for about five minutes; she then leant back in her seat and occasionally wrote on her pad, talking all the time. She told me the contents of my letter to Sir A. G.

The reply took one and one half hours to write; probably my changing the conditions in the room had some effect in delaying the writing. There was a note from Iola on the back of my short letter from Sir A. G. which referred to some chaff that occurred during the sitting with reference to certain erroneous spelling in a previous letter. On the outside of the envelope were the words, "From Sir A. G." in handwriting different to the above note and also to the writing of the reply letter. The signature of the latter bore some resemblance to that of my friend in earth life, but not sufficiently so as to be quite sure that it was his.

At 4 p.m. this letter was posted to Sir William Crookes.

On the same evening, January 21, 1909. I sat with May Bangs from 7.15 to 8.50 for a reply to a letter I had written in the afternoon to Cleopatra. The atmospheric conditions were bad. It was raining, and the air was heavy and close. This letter also occupied an hour and a half. The psychic sat in her usual place. As before, I used my own slates and bands. The conversation of May Bangs showed some knowledge of the contents of my letter, but not all.

My letter contained a request that Cleopatra would cause her portrait to be precipitated at 10.30 on the following morning, and began in this way: "Will you precipitate your portrait on the canvas tomorrow at 10.30, and will you add such words or signs as will be recognized by an experienced student of Egyptian history?

The following are extracts from the reply:

My good friend of earth. You have been told that I have come into your life for particular purposes, and it is true. A long, long time have I been on the spirit side of life. Ages it is if you calculate time, and during that period I have passed into realms far remote from earth. All that was near and dear to me of your sphere have long, long since joined me, and also advanced through numberless spheres. Truth is ever uppermost in the soul's ambition, and the time has come when mortals shall come further into the light. There are many mysteries that only spirits of a long time experience, and study can impart to those of your sphere with any degree of understanding and practical application. So it is that I have come into your life to aid in this very desirable work and I have chosen you as my subject through whom to work. I know of your earnest honest desire to fathom for yourself and the world this great momentous question. And I am bringing to you these different phenomena in evidence of my presence in introduction of my identity. I am very desirous to give you my portrait through this influence and the good artist that is also high and proficient in his art knowledge that you may know me better. And so from that chain of harmony and receptivity that will ensure the highest spiritual good. In brief, I desire to come to you through your own psychic power and receptivity that is gradually unfolding as you continue in your research.

I promise to come to you in likeness, dress, and all the characteristic emblems true to my native land of earth here that I am sure will be recognized by experienced students in Egyptian history...As you open the way, for the present all these wonderful experiences are for you alone. They will bring the truth and light in such a way that shall demonstrate to others, and make.....thought.

Yes, people of different spheres live together in spirit life. This truth I will explain to you again when better conditions and space affords opportunity. It is always most wise to anyone (?) in the morning hour for spirit phenomena, when the life current is at high tide, as it were.

...As you gain spiritual knowledge here so do you prepare yourself spiritually for a higher understanding in the life to come.

My good friend, I have not come to you at best this evening. I shall therefore ask another opportunity at your pleasure and convenience.

IN GUIDANCE, CLEOPATRA

Of course I am not in a position to assert that the Cleopatra of history wrote this letter. I cannot possibly tell whether it was a personation or not; I have no means of doing so. The immediate interest in the letter does not, in this case, lie in the identity of the writer, but in the nature of the ink with which it was written. The writing is not dissimilar to that in the reply from Sir A. G. It seems highly probable that all the letters are written, or precipitated, by the same spirit, "writing guide" of the psychic, whom the individuals on the other side use as we do a typist. The letter was mailed to Sir William Crookes the following morning, January 22nd.

I arrived at Rochester on February 6. On February 14, I received a letter from Sir William Crookes, dated 7 Kensington Park Gardens, February 4, 1909:

Dear Admiral Moore,

I received your interesting letter a few days ago, and at once tested the ink for lithium, with the following results:

A word was cut from sheet 4 of Sir G.'s letter, and it was burnt in the spectroscope. Abundant evidence of lithium was obtained. A blot of ink at the foot of the same sheet also contained much lithium. A piece of blank paper from the same sheet contained no lithium. A word from Sister's letter at the back of yours contained plenty of lithium. A piece of the picture of the hotel, in printing ink was cut from the heading of the paper. It contained no lithium.

The envelope addressed by you to yourself, having on it also the words "Communication from A .G." had the word "from" cut out, and also the word "Admiral" in Admiral Moore's own writing, cut out. These were tested in the spectroscope, with the result that the word "from" contained much lithium, while the word "Admiral" contained none at all.

I have this morning received the letter signed "Cleopatra"; the ink here also contains much lithium.

These results you may rely on as absolutely correct. Is it possible that some hint of adding lithium to ink has slipped out? May I suggest an experiment which may be useful? Go to the medium whence these letters were obtained, taking your own ink and other things apparently as before; but be very careful to have an ink that has no lithium in it. Get a letter as before, and let me test it for lithium. If the medium herself has been using ink which has lithium in it, she will use it again, and will be found out; but if she is genuine, there will be no lithium in the ink in which the letter is written.

When I reached home Sir William told me that some people imagined there was lithium in nearly everything. After he had finished his examination of the letters, he tested a piece of cigarette ash for lithium. It was found to contain it; but the lithium in the ink was certainly a thousand times as much as that in the ash.

The suggestion of again testing the medium, coming from so eminent an authority, was not to be ignored. I could not say for certain that before the second (the Cleopatra) letter was obtained I had not used the word "lithium." The psychic and I got by that time on the terms of fellow students, and she was as much interested as I was in the test. This much I knew: that if, perchance, I had let the word escape me, it would have conveyed nothing to her, and she could not have known where to get the citrate, nor, indeed, what to ask for. But, naturally, my mere assertion of this would not have satisfied Sir William.

Having plenty of time, I returned to Chicago (600 miles), and visited May Bangs on the morning of February 27, 1909, with every sign of wanting another test letter, taking my own materials, together with a small bottle of common ink. The sealed letter this time was written to a mutual friend of Sir William's and mine, and the usual four blank sheets of hotel paper were enclosed. The ink used in the reply has been found by Sir William to contain *no trace of lithium.*

I am greatly indebted to Sir William Crookes for kindly interesting himself in my investigations; his tests have enabled me to feel sure of my ground.

A professional, scientific explanation would have to come forward to destroy the superior level of evidence as demonstrated in this experiment.

Experiment with Spirit of Frederick W. H. Myers[13]

On March 2nd, I wrote a letter in my hotel to Mr. F. W. H. Myers, reminding him of his promise made in Rochester to endeavor to reply to a letter from me at the Bangs Sisters', at Chicago, and asking him to identify himself as far as he could for the benefit of his friends in England. The following was the reply found in a closed letter between the slates:

My good friend and Co-worker,

I greet you this evening and am very pleased to come to you. It is very kind of you to give opportunity of all these grand phenomena proving continued life after so-called death. It is indeed unfortunate that spirit is somewhat limited in power of expression; especially so when called upon to relate or recall some special event or circumstances occurring when in the earth form; this my good friend is due to the fact that the spirit is over-anxious to manifest in a way the mind suggests, the knowledge of which is perfectly clear to the spirit when in its free atmosphere - but when returning to manifest to mortals the atmosphere and all the conditions pertaining or surrounding to this life is so dense and clouded, that for the time being memory of these matter are renewed only as you make reference to them; thus again the Science of Spirit communicating with mortals is so intricate that it is quite difficult to master this alone, without entering into other branches; or is it designed by the Great overwhelming power, and that Intelligence men call God, that mortals should be able to penetrate all pertaining to this or higher life? Were it so, the people of Earth would become very dissatisfied with life, and more often tap (?) the time of their short stay, or, in other words, undo the set laws of Nature. Conviction is individual. Science in the material world can never reach a point of understanding to explain these things; it is utterly useless, but each member can receive and become satisfied to his or her own

---

[13] Frederick William Henry Myers (1843-1901) According to *The Encyclopedia of Psychic Science*: "A leading mind in psychical research, founder of a cosmic philosophy which may yet revolutionize scientific thought, a profound scholar, a poet of distinction and a brilliant psychologist." Myer's great work, *Human Personality and its Survival of Bodily Death*, published posthumously was, and always will be, a classic of psychical research.

understanding; this is all. However the law of evolution is carrying you onward and upward until you all feel a close correspondence in your own soul to the Great One's Soul, and little things like these manifestations do and will confound the mighty. Give my very best wishes to our great brother and co-worker Sir......, and also Sir......... I am with them heart and hand in this great cause and, though they have been able to reach the point where they can determine this question for the world, greater achievements are being made right away, until in a very short time sufficient evidence will be given that may be able to give to the world a clear solution that shall occasion mortals to accept it in great majority as a truth, absolutely fixed truths.

I urge you to continue in your research my friends. I find since entering this great world of worlds that I knew but little, nay nothing, in comparison with that which is to be known. I am still deeply interested in research and shall give you matters of interest from time to time, for our sensitives are growing more sensitive each day and this is the element required to give freedom of expression that brings evidence of identity.

Yours ever in the cause of all truth and light,

~ F.W.H.MYERS

We commenced to sit at 7.30 p.m. and at 8.05 p.m. the letter was finished. Lizzie Bangs joined us at 7.55 by request. On both sides of the outside of the envelope was a message from Iola about her portrait and other matters. The writing inside the envelope occupied six pages of hotel paper. It is in the same writing as other letters that I received through the mediumship of the Bangs Sisters. I have not the faintest idea whether it was dictated by Mr. Myers or not. There is nothing evidential in it. I did not know Mr. Myers; but he came to me, unasked, through Mrs. Georgia, at Rochester, and this led me to request him to correspond through the Bangs. It may have been dictated by some personating spirit, for they are legion. I have thought it best to record it, if only to show how much can be done in an hour. The style is not that of Myers, certainly; but in my opinion, the sentiments are above the modest conceptions of the normal Lizzie Bangs. Moreover, if we are to assume the possibility of the letter being juggled out of the room (which I do not), the time for writing the reply would have to be reduced to no less than forty minutes. Neither on this nor any other occasion was I able to detect any sign of the envelopes having been tampered with.

I have referred to three test-letters, two with lithium ink, on my first visit to Chicago, and one with ordinary ink, on my second visit. In the first of these letters there was a postscript from my guide Iola, alluding to some chaff that had taken place during that particular sitting. I had spoken to May Bangs (the only other person in the room), about some misspelt words in a previous letter which was also written by my guide or at her dictation, and the alleged writer vigorously defended herself. The doors of the room were always closed.

Again, when we sat for the last of the three letters, that on February 27, 1909, May Bangs asked me to cut off a small piece of wood, point it, and put it between the slates where the letter reposed; she thought the invisible writer would make use of it for her script. When the letter was finished, I was told not to open it. It was addressed across the flap to "Sir William Crookes, F. R. S." When it was opened by him in London, he found my piece of pointed wood inside the letter. It had been dipped in ink, and one word at the beginning had actually been written with the blunt instrument. The letter itself was feeble.

The concomitant evidence of the fact that no mortal had anything to do with the replies to my letters is strong. Several times references were made to conversations that took place across the table while the writings were in progress.

The following incidents will suffice to close the subject:

On Wednesday, March 3, from 11.15 a.m. to 12.15 p.m., I sat with May Bangs for a reply from Hypatia (spirit guide). During the sitting I told the medium that some gentleman in England had discussed with me the possibility of discovering if the ink on the slates was the identical ink used in the replies, by measuring the diminution of ink in the pot. My opinion was that we could not determine the question in this way, and May Bangs agreed with me. We were not using slates on this occasion, but had put the sealed letter under a stretched canvas; this was covered over by a cloth tucked in all around, and the ink was on top, not covered up. Immediately after May Bangs spoke (her hands were quite three feet from the ink, and we were sitting in full light), the ink fell in the pot. When the reply was finished, I found a communication from my guide outside the envelope referring to a matter, not the ink, which the psychic and I had been discussing a few minutes before. When I took away my letter, I was directed (through taps on the slates) to bring some flowers in the afternoon.

I must mention here that, after I began bringing my own materials, the slates used for communications by taps from the unseen were the Bangs' own slates. It is very necessary to make this clear, for the casual reader might suppose that the psychic and I held the slates, which contained the sealed letter.

At 4 p.m. of the same day I returned with another sealed letter, a tea-rosebud, and two pink carnations; these flowers I put into a glass vase nine inches high, nearly full of water. May Bangs and I sat for the reply to my letter at 5.10. It was broad daylight. My letter was under a stretched canvas, which was covered over with a red cloth tucked in all round. On top of it I placed my own little open tin pot full of common ink, bought in Van Buren Street two hours before, *and the corked ink-bottle.*

The rosebud opened soon after we sat down. At 5.30 the flowers began to jump about spasmodically in the vase, and worked themselves halfway round the rim. At 5.35 the tea-rose and one carnation were pulled down by invisible power towards the letter. Constant commotion was going on with the flowers in the water; ultimately the rose nearly wriggled itself out of the glass vase.

At 5.40 I said: "I never heard of any phenomenon of this kind being done if the eyes of the observers were concentrated on the object." The Bangs' slates were held between us, and the message rapped out, "Look out of the window." We both turned our heads simultaneously towards the window; instantly the vase upset away from the letter, the water was thrown upon the carpet, where it soon dried up, and the flowers disappeared.

At 5.42, as the light in the room was fading, I asked May Bangs to light the gas behind her; the window blind was still kept up.

At 5.48 my little pot of ink was nearly empty. I filled it up, by request, from the parent ink-bottle.

At 5.52 the ink bubbled away again. The pot being empty, I filled it up a third time. We were then told by impression, or by taps on the slate, to examine the parent bottle. I put some of the liquid in it on a piece of paper, and found that the essence had been extracted from it and that it was very watery.

At 5.56 the ink in the small pot was bubbling and getting lower and lower; at 6.00 it was dry. I filled it up for a fourth time.

At 6.05 taps announced that the letter was finished. On the outside of the envelope was written: "The remaining pink I claim to take with me, Iola." I slit open the letter at the top, and found inside the envelope: (a) My letter. (b) Reply of six pages, in which there was an allusion to the flower phenomenon described above. (c) The tea-rose, one carnation, and some leaves. Not a sign could I find in the room of the second carnation. I poured the ink from the little pot back into the ink-bottle, and again examined the contents of the bottle; there was nothing but dirty water. All the essence of the ink had been extracted, and an entire five-cent bottle of ink had been consumed in one sitting.

On the evening of March 5, 1909, I took a tea-rose, a carnation, and a letter to the Bangs' house. I wanted the flowers to be taken away by Iola as my parting present, for the next day I was leaving for England. If the invisibles could accomplish what they had done the previous evening, they would certainly be able to dematerialize these flowers. I was not disappointed; but the phenomenon was, in a measure, spoilt by the nervousness of May Bangs. I had frequently observed her on previous occasions; she was probably overworked. All psychics have their limitations, and possibly I ought to have known that such a delicate phenomenon should have not been started after a hard day's work. The flowers were placed in water in the same glass vase as was used before, and the vase put in the same position on the table, the letter being under a stretched canvas as before.

At 7.42 we sat for a reply to the letter, and with the hope that the flowers might be dematerialized.

At 8.00 the flowers began to shiver and jump a little, the water bubbling in the glass. The gas-jet was lowered and shaded from the vase, but there was enough light to see each other quite distinctly and all objects in the room. From the first, the psychic fixed her eyes on the vase. I begged of her to become less concentrated, as I feared a failure. By and by the rose lifted itself out of the glass, and May Bangs, apparently unable to control herself, reached forward and, with her hand, dashed it back into the glass with an excited gesture. I thought the experiment had failed; but no, the two flowers still showed signs of animation, and kept on waggling to and fro, and apparently becoming smaller. I seized the glass vase with my left hand for some minutes. A message came by impression through May Bangs: "Put the vase on your side of the shelf of the table." At 8.15 I placed it almost touching my right leg under the table, on the shelf, well out of sight and reach of the psychic. At 8.20 May Bangs opened a door and shouted for her sister Lizzie to come into the room to assist by her power. At 8.28 a message came to turn up the light, which was done by May Bangs. I lifted the vase; the water was there, *but the flowers had disappeared.*

At 8.31 the usual taps announced that the reply to the letter was finished. The little pot (this time underneath the frame) was examined, and all the ink in it had dried up.

This was the only manifestation and want of self control of May Bangs on this occasion, when a fine manifestation was partially spoilt, may be accounted for by an incident that took place later in the afternoon, and which must have taxed the mediumistic powers of two sisters to the utmost.

In recent times no psychics have been so long and so constantly under fire of criticism as the Bangs Sisters. I record the fact, but entirely without surprise. The manifestations which appear through their mediumship are of such a startling nature as to render it in the highest degree improbable that anyone, however experienced he may be as an investigator, can credit the accounts of what takes place, unless he has actually seen the various phenomena that occur. Many have been the efforts to show that what happens in their presence is the effect of pure conjuring on their own part. *All have failed.*

"The theory of fraud set up to account for the replies to letters in sealed envelopes is that the letter is got out from between the slates or from under the stretched frame; then passed out of the closed room under a door, opened, answered normally by Lizzie Bangs or some other confederate, and returned the same way. The ink is likewise conveyed from the room. I say that, under the circumstances in which I sat with May Bangs, such a feat of conjuring was *impossible*. In eight cases out of twelve she had no opportunity of touching the letters or the ink. Any attempt to tamper with slates, stretched canvas, or ink would have resulted in the spilling of the ink; sometimes I used five rubber bands; on three occasions the ink was in sight, and only one foot fifteen inches from me. In all cases the slates or stretched canvas were nearer to me than the psychic. For the moment, however, let us suppose that this was the *modus operandi*. We have yet to account for allusions in the letters to conversations at the table during the séance, and to the knowledge possessed by May Bangs (the only other person in the room) of the contents of my letter. In at least six cases she told me the chief points (sometimes everything) of my own script while we were sitting at the table.

The Bangs are not always successful. As far as I could judge, the phenomena generally occurred when the sitter was positive, like myself—a person wholly devoid of any receptive mediumistic faculty. Their time is fully occupied; I was only one of many visitors. They offered every facility for examination of the premises, and I roamed through their rooms alone for at least a quarter of an hour, on the average, every day I was in Chicago.

MARGUERITE HUNTER

I have in my library a rare book, 254 pages, published in 1894 by C. H. Horine, and the entire work was written through the independent slate writing of Miss Lizzie Bangs.

Illustrated in this book are photographs from the book of the very slates that were used for the dedication of the work, and I have transcribed what they said, along with the information written about the methodology used in the sittings. With all the information I have had at hand regarding the Bangs, this is the only slate writing of theirs that has been photographed and reprinted that I know of. Of interest is the fact that also used for the production of this book was Alan Campbell, one of the famous Campbell Brothers. The vernacular is lofty and typical of ministering spirits of the day.

Dedication

This book is dedicated by its author in the spirit world to humanity, and written through spirit and medial power substantially as it was dictated. For this purpose and to further the spread of truth she has, through the influence of a cooperative spirit band acting in harmony with chosen media of the earth plane, organized forces sufficient to perfect her design. The author herself, a noble woman, after varied and deep experiences, not only in the joyous expression of youth but in the sadness which often fringes with tragic shadows the events of life, but comparatively a few years ago passed to the brighter scenes and spheres beyond. A humanitarian by nature, she is still humanly interested in the progress of the human race. Her recollection of earth events has not faded, her affection and sympathy for human kind have not been obliterated by the change called death. She is a bright intelligence, a soul transferred from the earth life to a higher spiritual plane, and what she says may be accepted as authority on the subject which she treats. She, however, submits the narrative of her life and the knowledge which she has acquired of the soul and its law of unfoldment to the critical and searching analysis of human reason and science, and wishes in no other way than by the unimpeachable authority of truth as taught in her narrative to reach the end for which she sends the book out into the world. Her own people, for whose mental and spiritual awakening she first conceived the purpose of the book, and deeply religious as they regard religion, are supremely honest in their convictions, but they are not investigators or disciples of the science, philosophy and religion of Spiritualism. They do not, therefore, believe in spirit manifestations nor spirit communion, but abide by the faith of the orthodox Christian. Without giving any offense or attempting to bring to light any facts of a personal and family nature that might be regarded as irrelevant to the work, or a breach of family and social etiquette, yet she has woven into the narrative unmistakable signs of her identity which they will not fail to recognize and understand, and all that she gives she imprints with the same personality and dignity of spirit that characterized her life and career.

The object of the narrative as thus arranged and composed is to present to them and others, first the thought of everlasting unity of the soul in all expressions here and in the eternal spheres, and then the collateral and contingent lessons out-wrought by every bright or sad, trifling or solemn, ignoble or noble, revengeful or loving thought and deed, all of which go to make the quality of the soul's spirituality as well as the spheres which it inhabits. Thus, as the foundation of the temple is related to the massive and beautiful edifice, or the external form discloses as a symbol the interior grandeur and points to the gracious simplicity of the inner shrine and holy of holies, so all that occurs in and of the material life, shapes and tends to elaborate the real design of the soul, which matter and force and the form, in the physical, mental and spiritual life as constituting the soul's environment and embodiment, ever serve and unfold. Thus she shows and thus she elaborates the law and conditions and her advancement and elevation. She has no other purpose in translating the book to the earth-form and to earth's children, than that, by it and the elucidation of the principles and facts contained in it, she might lead them, her immediate kinsfolk and all who may heed and profit by these lessons, out of a blind credulity, an obsolete and despiritualizing faith and an unreasonable and unscientific religion to the truth that alone maketh free, away from the letter that killeth to the Spirit that giveth life.

Spiritual life is more than assent to creeds and dogmas or a mere conformity to moral rules and ethical codes. It is the character which is the result of that aspirational nature, inflowing and outflowing with the power of the spirit in saintly communion with the angelic hosts, that illumines the face with the beatific smile and glorifies the inner life with love, harmony and peace. Thus she would inspire in their and all souls such ardent aspiration and kindle the fires that flame forth a radiance which, as the candle placed upon the stand, gives light to all that come within the circumference of its aura.

She wishes to add as a final word that many spirit intelligences have aided her in thought and influence to complete this, her chosen work.

E. UNITY, THE SPIRIT BAND

Concerning the independent writing on slates necessary for the full book, it was said the medium, Lizzie S. Bangs, received from six to eight full written slates at each of the sittings, Mr. Horine holding the slates with the medium. These sittings were held three times a week and were begun in November, 1893, and were ended April 28th, 1894.

There is also another book, *Through the Valley of the Shadow and Beyond*, 1908, said by its copyright owner, Dr. C. H. Carson, that it too was entirely dictated through the independent writing of the Bangs Sisters, 339 pages.

Quote:

In the minds of many people mediumistic phenomena are associated with fraud, credulity and deception; and unfortunately, there is a good deal of reason for this, because very many mediums have been accused of fraud, and often apparently with justice. Fraudulent mediums, however, are not so numerous as skeptics allege; the notion arises, no doubt, from the fact that, while ordinary people hear nothing of the many honest ones, all the world hears is those who are accused or convicted of fraud. Rogues and cheats are to be found in every walk of life. The Church, Law, and Medicine are all disgraced occasionally by the conviction of disreputable practitioners, but, however numerous the delinquents, their conviction is never used as an argument against the usefulness or importance of the profession they have disgraced. In contrast, the fraudulent medium is often urged by skeptics as an argument against Spiritualism and the reality of mediumistic phenomena.

~ A. Campbell Holmes

REV. STANLEY L. KREBS

This article, mentioned in the Introduction, is based on information published in the Proceedings for the American Society of Psychical Research, 1901.

Around 1900, Rev. Stanley L. Krebs, an English psychic investigator, as he called himself, made an appointment to sit with the Bangs Sisters so he could determine their method of slate-writing.

According to Krebs, the Bangs Sisters asked him to bring with him to the sitting a sealed envelope containing a letter he had written to a deceased friend, along with blank paper for a reply. To be certain of a "Sherlock Holmes" approach to this situation, Krebs brought with him, according to his statements in his report to the S.P.R., a small mirror, which he positioned in his lap once he was seated at the séance' table, giving him an "excellent view of any trickery occurring below the tabletop."

Lizzie Bangs then sandwiched Krebs' letter between two slates and tied them with twine, but, when she briefly turned her back, Krebs slyly examined the slates and discovered that the medium had slid a small wedge between them so it would open a small "gap" between them. When Lizzie turned back, Krebs, with his Sherlock Holmes mirror, then saw her pick up the slates (right in front of him?) and drop the letter from between the slates - through the opening - onto her lap. All the while this dubious act was happening he was, he wanted the readers to believe, staring at his lap (mirror) watching her.

Then, as Lizzie Bangs, according to Krebs, "attempted to distract him by making wild guesses about his dead friend's name" he saw her, "bend down (again, right in front of him?) and place the letter onto a sort of small, dark colored tray on a long handle, which was then drawn backward under the door behind the medium."

Of course, Krebs then insinuated in his story that May Bangs who, he assumed, was hiding behind this door, then unsealed or steamed open the letter, read it, then sent a message out to Lizzie Bangs by way of the long handled tray. This message was a small piece of paper which Lizzie Bangs, while pretending to shift in her chair, bent down and picked up, placed on her lap and, according to Krebs, "quickly read." This little slip supposedly contained the spirit names that May Bangs had written down behind the door after first reading Krebs' letter. Lizzie then began reciting the names of these spirits to Krebs so he would think that his spirit friends were there. He then goes on to say that after several minutes he, "spied his original letter being secretly slid back into the room, picked up by Lizzie, then, under more "distractions," slid it back between the slates and removed the secret wedge between the slates. She then allowed Krebs to untie the slates, open his "sealed" letter, and read the spirit messages on the papers which had—in his mind—to have been written by May Bangs. This is what he actually said he witnessed. I wonder why May Bangs would need to hide behind a door to answer, through clairvoyance I might add, questions from the sitters? The emphasis being put on the fraudulent practice of the Bangs slate writing seems to neglect the fact that the answers from the spirits were, invariably, always correct.

Independent Writing: Admiral Moore - continued....
January 1911

> My readers will forgive me for not disclosing the measurements and all other particulars of the Bangs Sisters' séance room, or the nature of the chemical I took from England to prove that the ink used in the reply letter was the same ink as I put on or near the slates. I have good reason for not doing so, in view of the statements made in an article published in The Annals of Psychical Science, June to September, 1910.

> (THIS MUST HAVE BEEN ANOTHER CHEMICAL EXPERIMENT; HE HAD MENTIONED LITHIUM CITRATE BEFORE IN JANUARY 21ST, 1909 - ED)

Continuing:

> On Monday, January 30, I bought two hinged school-slates and six broad India-rubber bands. The ink, to be put on the table, had been purchased in England; also a chemical that would speedily and effectively prove whether the ink with which the reply letter was written was my ink or not. I took with me a short letter, written in England, which contained one question: two blank sheets were enclosed for

reply; all these were placed in one envelope, sealed in such a manner as to defy its being opened without detection. Thus equipped, and carrying some flowers, I attended the Bangs' house at the appointed time - 11 a.m. Lizzie Bangs did not appear till 11.45, when we sat. I had moved the table close up against the center of the west wall. I placed May Bangs on the north side of the table with directions not to move her chair close up to it, and requested Lizzie to sit in a chair in the south-east corner of the room, and some four to five feet from me. I sat, with my back to the light, on the south side of the table, with my left shoulder against the west door. From this position I could see the hall and door into May Bangs' house, for I threw open the north door of the séance room, and also the east door (that which leads into Lizzie Bangs house), which is the alleged object of suspicion.

My letter was put between the slates, and Lizzie Bangs held one corner which I stretched three rubber bands around them lengthways and three crossways; then I laid them on a table, a little my side of the center, put a small pot in the center of the top, filled it more than half full with my ink, and surrounded it with a black cloth, stretching to the edge of the slates. Everything was a casual as possible. Mrs. Bangs (Meroe, the mother) wandered in an out of the room; occasionally a dog or two would pass through. May Bangs frequently left her chair and the room; Lizzie left her chair only, at my request, to wind up the gramophone, which played nearly the whole time. If May Bangs drew up her chair to the table, she was put back. From the first to last May Bangs did not touch the slates or the little inkpot. The parent bottle of ink was in my pocket. Conversation was going on all the time. We talked principally of the S.P.R. Report that I had given to the sisters the previous night. Lizzie Bangs had, I think, heard of it, because she told me amusing stories of its author. May had not heard of it - she never reads anything. Certainly the author had not sent them a copy of the pamphlet, which was published in England.

Imagine the conditions: Table shifted to a part of the room to which it was a stranger; the psychic, who functions alone in the phenomenon of writing within sealed envelopes at the usual sittings for this purpose, placed with her face towards the southern light streaming into the room; both woman seething with indignation at cowardly attacks published in England; the suspected door wide open; the door into the hall wide open; and Lizzie, the person who, it is alleged, hides behind the suspected door and writes the replies, in the room. (Interesting that Rev. Stanley Krebs' report said that it was May Bangs hiding behind the door – Ed.).

Lizzie said to me: "You have no idea how this sudden and complete upset of our usual conditions affects us. We have no objection to a gradual altering of our accustomed habits; for instance, investigators may come and take us on the first day as we usually sit (in the case of this phenomenon I should not be here, but doing other work); on the second day a slight alteration would be made, at the suggestion of the investigators; on the third say another item would be changed; on the fourth another - and so on, until every phase of our usual conditions was altered. But to come suddenly upon us and change all our conditions in one day is more than any sensitive can stand - the strain is too great. If you had not told me of these slanders, I assure you I would never have consented to your demands. We will never do it again for anyone.

To this I replied: "I knew I should not be able to get this test unless I gave you sound reasons for it. You are suspected of sitting, or crouching, behind that door (pointing to it), listening, and answering the letters passed out to you by your sister. I know it is untrue, and, moreover, impossible, as I examined this room in 1909, and again a few days ago; the thing cannot be done. But we must finish this test. I cannot spend more than a day or two here. I have confidence that we shall succeed."

It is a fact that all through this troublesome work I felt a certainty of success. Perhaps this feeling was partly due to the recollection of my work with these true psychics in 1909.

At 12.20 the sisters went down to dinner separately, some food being brought out to me in the séance-room where I sat controlling the slates. The spirits encouraged my smoking on every occasion, and I must have got through a good many cigars. At 1.20 we sat again in the same seats, May Bangs, as restless as ever, seldom remaining in her chair for more than a few minutes. At 2.15 a message came: "You are too intent; it would be better to postpone the sitting until tomorrow." Question: "How are you getting on?" Answer: "Slow, but sure." I packed up my slates in paper, tied them up with a cord, and took them back to my hotel where they were locked up. The little ink pot was emptied and washed out by me. On future days the slates were not removed from the paper, except on one occasion; and the small pot was not used; my travelling bottle of ink was unscrewed, and the cork taken out.

Second day - Tuesday, January 31.

We sat under precisely the same conditions as before, from 11.00 to 1.25. Once May Bangs demanded to see the letter, saying, "How do I know if anything is within the slates?" The slates were then opened by myself, the sisters not touching them; and when May Bangs was satisfied by seeing the letter, I put the rubber bands on as before, and tied the slates up in paper. As usual, the gramophone was played, and the two doors were wide open. May Bangs again complained: "These conditions are all wrong; we cannot go on like this; I ought to touch the slates." I answered: "Very well, you shall, if the controls advise us to let you do so. Hold this slate (one belonging to the Bangs Sisters); I will take the other end." We took the Bangs' slate between us. Vigorous rapping was heard, and the sisters interpreted, "It is not necessary." With this the psychic was satisfied. At 12.05 we were told again that we were "too intent; no writing had been accomplished, but the slates were being surrounded with the necessary magnetism. We were to walk about and change vibrations." As May Bangs had important legal business in the city, and Lizzie had many letters to write, we separated till 7.00 p.m., I, of course, taking my slates and ink to my hotel. I found diversion in some business matter I had to attend to in town.

At 7.00 p.m. we sat again. I arrived a few minutes before, and questioned May Bangs as to her little outing, inquiring especially if she had derived any benefit from the fresh air. Then out came a story of incredible folly. After I had left the house, a man, evidently in distress, was let in, and implored by May Bangs to give him a sitting for a letter. She refused him twice, having her business in view; but, as he was turning away from the door, with obvious keen disappointment in his face, she relented. One letter answered, she functioned for another. Then it was too late to do her business in town; a second man came in, and she sat for him also. I was indignant. Both the sisters admitted the mistake, May Bangs saying: "Well, Mr. Moore, I know it was wrong; but when I saw tears in that man's eyes I couldn't help it, and that is all there is about it."

My slates, wrapped in paper, were placed in the usual position on the table, my hand upon them. In a minute or two we were told that the power of the psychic had been exhausted during the afternoon, and that it was not a good sitting. No writing had yet been done, but progress had been made during the day in surrounding the slates with the necessary force to meet the altered conditions. For the third time I walked off with my slates and ink.

Third day - Wednesday, February 1, 1911

We met in the séance room at 11 a.m. I was told that friends were coming about noon, but we hoped the reply to my letter would be finished before that. Conditions as before; doors thrown open, gramophone playing, and both psychics present. May Bangs somewhat less restless. At 11.55, no signal having been given to open the slates, I asked: "When the visitors come, may they sit with us?" Answer: "We cannot tell till they are in the room; they are now outside." Immediately there was a ring at the front door, and Mrs. Bangs let in a gentleman and a lady. The Bangs Sisters went out to meet them and I followed, after picking up my slates and ink. There was an interval of half an hour, during which time we all talked in Lizzie Bangs' drawing room. The lady visitor told me they had 'phoned' for a sitting on the previous afternoon. Both she and her husband would gladly assist me and wait for their own business.

We all sat round the séance table, and I again put my slates and ink on top of it in the same position as before, with one hand upon them. The chemical I had brought from England remained throughout all the sittings in the left pocket of my coat. At 12.40 Lizzie Bangs went down to dinner, and the restless May sat part of the time with the visitors and myself around the séance table, and then went to her meal or walked about the house. I smoked and chatted with the visitors, who, I found were both mediumistic.

A little after 1.00 p. m., the party of five assembled round the table. At 1.20 May Bangs said excitedly: "If this thing does not come off now, I refuse to sit again; I felt as if I was being torn to pieces." A message came: "The visitors are to go into the front parlour; the psychics and you (that was me) into the back drawing room, which is to be darkened. You are to take your slates and ink with you." No need to tell me that! Accordingly, the visitors departed to the front parlour, and the Bangs Sisters went with me into the neighboring room; this room was darkened with the shutters, but there was enough light left for me to see the white paper in which the slates were tied up, in front of me, with one of my hands on them. The open bottle of ink was at my left elbow, Lizzie Bangs about two feet to my left, May in an easy chair some six or seven feet away. After five minutes Lizzie and I saw lights, from the size of half-a-dollar to that of a dollar, come and go round and behind the head of May Bangs. Later a faint ethereal form rose behind her. I was not able to see what this phantom did to the psychic, but it remained a few minutes, and at 1.45 she said she felt much better; we were told to separate and divert ourselves, but not to assemble in the séance room for an hour.

I screwed up my ink-bottle, took my slates, and entered into conversation with the gentleman in the front parlour, who diverted my attention by relating to me a most interesting story of his conversion to spiritualism. Lizzie Bangs' attention was taken off from the test by entertaining a lady in her own drawing room, and May Bangs wandered round the séance table. I laid the slates down and opened my ink, till then in my pocket. About 3.10 the message came: "We are making his chemical to work in the opposite way to what he intends." At 3.20 came the welcome order to "open the slates."

I removed the paper cover, took off the rubber bands, and opened the hinged slates. The letter had not been tampered with. I cut it open, and observed that on the second sheet (i.e., the first intended for a reply) a portion in the center of the first page looked as if it had some sort of scratchy writing on it; it then looked different from what it did when I had put it in at home. I was directed to try my chemical on the blank one-third of the page on which the question was written, and I also applied it to the one-third of a page of the suspicious looking second sheet. When the first was dry, we found the following, in very faint characters, like milk-writing, but quite unmistakable when the heat was applied:

"Let this prove to you my presence here today"- Iola

When we made ourselves quite sure of this writing, I examined the second sheet, and found a private message of four lines, in deep black characters, the writing being similar to that generally in evidence in all of the Bangs Sisters' reply letters. When I applied the chemical on it (I had already applied it under it), the test showed it was written with my ink. There was no reply to the question in my letter. The slates, ink, and chemical were under my control entirely throughout the three days of the experiment.

The last duty was to examine the houses, and to sit close to the alleged incriminating door, on the outside, and try if I could hear conversation in the séance room. The visitors and one of the Bangs Sisters talked in the middle of the séance room. I found it easy to detect that they were conversing in ordinary voices, but I only made out two words in a conversation of 'four or five minutes' duration.

So ended a trying ordeal of five days. Both sisters were much exhausted. May Bangs could hardly stand, and Lizzie, though calm, had evidently reached the limits of endurance. I was considerably depleted, and left for the East the next morning.

It is necessary for me to deal with the following statements in the article in The Annals of Psychical Science, already referred to: (1) That there is "a wide slit in the door" (p.449). There is no slit in any door, nor was there in 1909. (2) "I afterwards discovered several tiny pinholes in the strip of wood dividing the windows." (p.452). There is only one window. If the author means "sashes," there is no strip of wood in sight dividing the sashes; there is, however, something else which he has failed to notice, but nothing suspicious. It is the same now as in 1909. At the present juncture it would be unwise to give away more about the room. But I must state this as my conviction; either the author of that article has never been inside the Bangs' house, or is incapable of making ordinary observations with accuracy. The attack on these psychics, without sending them a copy, and in an English magazine which he knew they could not see, is an act that requires no comment from me. It may be left with safety to the judgment of my readers.

- ADMIRAL USBORNE MOORE

Although I do not agree in the least with the theories of David Abbott concerning the process of precipitated portraits, it is, nonetheless, the most thought out and thorough of all theories indicating, in his mind, how the process was carried out by the Bangs Sisters. Credit is due to him for the exhaustive work he did and the depth in which he believed in himself.

DAVID ABBOTT & HEREWARD CARRINGTON
SOME CONTROVERSIAL ISSUES EXPLORED
EXCERPTS FROM THE SPIRIT PORTRAIT MYSTERY: ITS FINAL SOLUTION
By David Phelps Abbott, Chicago, The Open Court Publishing Co., 1913. (33pp.)

Here is how I would do it if I were a lady medium. I should wear a skirt that was really open in front but lapped over in a fold; and I should suspend the portrait on a hanger between my legs under my skirt. If I were quite large I could carry a good-sized portrait here unobserved by all.

- DAVID P. ABBOTT

David Abbott:

It is now about four years since I made the discovery that finally cleared up one of the greatest of mediumistic mysteries. For about fifteen years the feat of producing spirit portraits has baffled all of the investigators that have studied the problem. Through its agency some of our most prominent men have been converted to spiritualism, and conjurers have universally acknowledged it to be the most miraculous phenomenon that ever confronted them. Meanwhile two famous lady mediums of Chicago have continued to produce these wonderful portraits as the work of the spirit world; and while many have disputed the genuineness of this claim without being able to substantiate their view, the large majority that were conversant with the subject have continued to be believers. Editor Francis of the "Progressive Thinker," a leading spiritualist journal, for years kept a standing cash offer to be given to anyone who could explain this wonder; but there were none who could do so, and he finally died without anyone claiming the reward.

Since the discovery of the secret of these productions, the illusion has been presented from the theatrical stage as a magical creation. The

English conjurer, Selbit, under authority of Dr.Wilmar of London (to whom I had sent the secret), first toured England and France with it, and then presented it on the Orpheum Circuit in America at a large salary. The great American magician, Mr. Howard Thurston, under direct authority from the writer, has now presented it in his programs for two years, and is still doing so; while Henry Clive, the English conjurer, and W. J. Nixon, known as the " Master Mind of Modern Magic," both are now presenting it in vaudeville houses in the east. I am informed that it is also being presented in Australia. The Pittsburg Post of Jan. 1, 1913 contained an offer of five hundred dollars made by Mr. Clive for any chemist who would chemically analyze his canvases and find them prepared in any way. These two last-named gentleman have had a controversy recently through Variety, as to who has the American rights, etc., and it has developed in this that salaries as high as five hundred dollars a week are now being paid in vaudeville for it. But this amount is small when compared with the sums paid to mediums for this work.

In the summer of 1908 the two Chicago mediums, above mentioned, visited Kansas City, MO., for a few months. It was said that their expenses were paid by a noted healer of that city, who usually had some fifty patients at his door each morning awaiting the "laying on of hands." He was said to have an income of five hundred dollars daily, and was Kansas City's heaviest individual bank depositor.

Mr. C. F. Eldredge of Kansas City, MO., in a letter speaking for the healer and these mediums, said: "I hope you will expose this work, for it is the greatest mystery in the world. One man of this city spent perhaps ten thousand dollars with these people, and he is today just as certain that his pictures were painted by spirit artists as that he lives. He has just published a big book on the subject,[14] all full of these pictures, which he claims was written by his dead wife through their mediumship. He is only one of hundreds who are ready to stake their lives on their work."

Mr. Eldredge is a very intelligent man, and is teaching the mysteries of the human mind, how to effect certain marvelous cures, and how

---

[14] Through the Valley of the Shadow and Beyond, by Rose M. Carson, copyright by C. H. Carson, 1908. Rose Carson was the spirit writer.

to perform other mental miracles - if I may be allowed the word. It was through a description furnished by him that I was able finally to work out the solution of this mystery, and to settle the extravagant claims of the mediums, besides making the stage illusion possible. Mr. Eldredge had the privilege of witnessing one of the Kansas City séances, and I here give his report:

Having met by appointment at the residence of the mediums, my doctor friend and myself were ushered into the studio where the sitting took place. The object was to secure a portrait in colors of the doctor's sister who was killed some six years ago in a runaway accident.

The doctor was requested by the mediums to select two canvases from a dozen or more that were leaning against a wall. This he did from near the middle of the pile, holding them up to the light and rubbing his hand over them in order to determine if there was any coating or film over them. I also examined them very carefully, and was satisfied there was not. One of the mediums now took the two framed canvases and, placing them face to face, stood them upon a small table in front of a window which looked out upon the Paseo, one of the great boulevards of our city. The canvases were leaned up against the window which faced the south.

One of the mediums stood upon a chair and pulled down the blind to the top of the canvases, and then each of them drew a soft, dark curtain from the side of the window to the frames, thus darkening all of the window except where the light came through the canvases.

The light from the window passed directly through the canvases and they appeared clear and white. My friend held a picture of his dead sister in his hand, being requested to fix the expression of her face in his mind. We were seated immediately in front of the window, not more than three feet from the canvases while the mediums stood at the two sides of the table holding them and talking to us.

After waiting possibly five minutes, one of the mediums said, "You will observe how the canvases are drawing. They are being sized." The front canvas did seem to be stretching on the frame making a slight noise, as if the thumb were being drawn upon the side of the frame. Presently the noise stopped, and there appeared on the outer edge of the canvases, or rather between the two, a slight shadow. I did not notice it until our attention was called to it by the mediums. It continued to darken while the center remained white and clear. It seemed like the glow of sunrise, but there was no form. Next we noticed an outline. The face was forming. We noticed two dark blurs that grew more distinct, and we saw that they were eyebrows and eyelashes of closed eyes. The lines of the mouth appeared, and the outlines of the head became visible, while the shoulders were distinct; and then the eyes opened out, giving a life-like effect to the portrait.

Was I dreaming? I felt like pinching myself to see. A woman's face was looking at us from between the canvases, beautiful in form and feature.

My friend had been told to suggest any changes he wanted during the formation of the picture. He now said that he would like the face turned a little more to the right giving more of a front view. Almost immediately the picture began to fade from the canvas, and it grew fainter until it lost every detail. The outlines of the head became indistinct. The eyes went out into mere dark rings. Presently we saw the face coming as before. The face seemed turned a little this time, though I am not positive that it was. I imagined that it was, and the doctor seemed better satisfied; however, the change was very slight, if any. We were so carried away with the marvel of the performance, that reason gave way to sentiment. The very marvel was inspiring. This time the development was more rapid. The eyes opened again as before.

The doctor now asked that the eyes be made a little darker blue, more of a gray and, while he was speaking, I noticed that the eyes were changing to blue gray, or else my imagination was playing me false. He now suggested a slight change of the nose, which was made, and the lines of the mouth were altered as his suggestion. He now suggested the face was a little too full, and it seemed to narrow slightly. The picture seemed to follow the doctor's thought. He was asked if he would have, as a hair ornament a crescent, a star or crown. The doctor suggested a crescent, and immediately a crescent of gold with gems of white appeared. Up to this time the shoulders seemed bare. He was asked to choose whether there should be a high or low collar. He suggested one of medium height and it at once appeared. On looking at the photograph, the doctor now saw a string of beads around the neck. Without speaking, the beads came into view about the neck, one bead at a time. They changed in color from white to amber then to gold. He seemed to conjure the picture. As a dream follows the will, so this picture followed the doctor's thought. Meanwhile the background had changed in color several times, from white to light yellow, then to dark yellow or brown, and then to green with a tinge of red, after which it mottled beautifully until the effect was superb. The changes took place like waves of light passing upwards over the whole picture. The two canvases were now laid flat on the table, and a third canvas was then lifted from the floor and placed over them for a cover. We were then asked to place our hands on this, so as to 'set the colors.' Soon the portrait was uncovered, and I found the paint was a kind of greasy substance, as I rubbed some of it on my fingers.

My friend had enclosed a photograph of his sister, together with a letter to her spirit, between slates for a time, in the presence of these mediums, some three days before this sitting. It was then his appointment was made.

I have heard of the Hindu magician who plants a seed and grows a tree before our eyes, and the turning of water into wine, but here was a phenomenon even greater; one that seemed to contradict every known law of nature; and now as I record this the day after, I am more bewildered than when I saw the work done. I do not believe the picture was painted before our eyes, for that is beyond rational belief, and by no process of reasoning can such an idea satisfy my mind. Where did the colors come from? How did they get between the close fitting canvases, and by what miraculous power were they intelligently spread over one of them?

We compared the portrait with the photograph; the psychics asked to see it, claiming never to have seen it before. The likeness was perfect. Anyone could recognize it. There seemed to have been no opportunity for trickery or fraud, and everything was open and above board. We could see all over the room at all times, under the table in front of us, and everywhere. Yet the work was contrary to natural law and all human experience.

Abbott:

Readers of my book Behind the Scenes with the Mediums, 1909, will remember some correspondence I had through The Open Court, January and May, 1907, in regard to some spirit portraits produced by certain famous mediums. At that time the descriptions of the act, as furnished me, were very meager and incomplete; and this fact misled me. Naturally, I thought of the old spray method of developing a prepared canvas, and elaborated on the method, thinking that I surely had the principle upon which the act was performed.

On August 11, 1909, which was nearly six months after my discovery, Dr. Wilma (William Marriott,) psychic investigator and lecturer, of 84 Bushwood Road, Kew, London S.W., wrote me a letter of inquiry, which I still have and of which I have furnished to the editor of "The Open Court," a photographic copy. ... I replied to this letter on August 25, 1909 and gave him all of the reports of the work then in my possession, and I also freely explained to him the principle which I had discovered for causing the portrait to materialize and dematerialize.

It will be remembered that in my early reports but one canvas was said to be used, and this was set in a window; but as soon as I learned that two canvases were used and faced together, I knew that a spray developer could not be employed, and I began to search for some other means.

Abbott had previously published in 1907, Behind the Scenes with the Mediums, stating then that an old "spray method of developing a prepared canvas" was used in spirit precipitated portraits and this - it must be inferred - was aimed directly at the Bangs Sisters.
He then went on to say in The Spirit Portrait Mystery:

However, as at a later date, I was furnished the above accurate reports of this remarkable performance, which showed entirely different conditions from those the first reports conveyed to my mind. I soon discovered that the spray method was impossible; and I freely confess that the explanation given in my book is not the correct one.

Abbott:

I also knew that in tricks every little thing is for a purpose, and that nothing superfluous is used when the art is perfect. I analyzed and re-analyzed the problem, and decided that there was certainly a good reason for using two canvases. Why did the mediums invariably use two faced together? Surely it would be much more simple as well as conclusive if but one were used. Also, if it were possible to produce a portrait when using but one, we certainly would hear of their doing it that way sometimes. Yes, there was a reason for using two canvases; and it surely was merely to have the front one conceal from the sitter what happened to the one behind it. When both were in position in the window, and the side and upper curtains drawn and pinned to the front frame, anything could happen to the rear canvas and the sitter would know nothing of it. Again, there must be a reason for laying the canvases over on the table and covering them with a third canvas under the pretense of "setting the colors." What could be the real reason of this? It will be seen later why this is. I was entirely satisfied that a painting was made in advance; and that somewhere before delivery of the portrait at the close of the séance, it was substituted or introduced in some way. I knew that in magic, substitutions always take place early in the performance - much earlier than one imagines - and hence the real trick is always expected sooner than is thought.

Now, evidently the portrait was really produced on the rear canvas, and it surely was in the window at the time the two were laid over on the table. So it must have been substituted before this time. Then it must really have been in the window during the entire coming and going effects. Laying them over on the table would bring it on top to be handed out first. How did it get in the window, and above all, how was it made to appear and disappear at will?

Abbott's continuing fixation on the canvases being laid on a table afterwards and then covered by another, was only evident in a few recorded instances of the precipitation process. The numerous eyewitness testimonies in Chapter 3 will bear this out.

Abbott:

Window traps permitting substitutions being impossible, and projection ideas and developers being out of the question, what subtle principle could here be involved? The more I thought, the greater the mystery became; and I finally decided that to take the advice of my friend, Mr. Rasgorshek, and experiment, was the only thing to do. I secured a portrait and a blank canvas, and as I had heard rumors that a graduated silk gauze was secretly introduced gradually between the canvases for screening off the portrait, I decided to try this. I made a rectangular frame that was only one eighth of an inch thick and placed it on rollers and a windlass, so that I could reel up many thicknesses of silk on it. This I placed between the two canvases in the window and began reeling. I did not decide where I would conceal my assistant, or how to get rid of the frame or substitute the portrait; I simply wanted to discover how to materialize and dematerialize the latter.

I then removed the frame from between the canvases and crowded them closer together; and the portrait, viewed from the front through blank canvas, immediately became clear and sharp. I again moved the portrait backward, viewing it through the front one. It grew indistinct, more and more "out of focus" until it became an indistinct cloud, then merely some dim shadows, and finally it vanished utterly leaving the canvas clear and white. I brought it forward slowly, and it gradually made its appearance, the dark lines first appearing, then the rosy glow at the center, and finally the features began to form; and at last the eyes changed from dark shadowy rings, to open, bright eyes.

I looked in awe. Here was the very thing for which I was searching, and without the screen or graduated gauze, or apparatus. Here was the long-sought subtle principle, the famous secret that had baffled scientists and the investigators of the world; and it was a thing so simple that it staggered me. When the canvases were separated, the rays of light passing through the portrait began to diverge and spread evenly over the blank canvas, until, as the distance was sufficiently increased between them, the illumination became evenly diffused over it. This distance was about three inches. At the same time, as the canvases were separated, side light was being admitted between them which helped to illuminate the front canvas evenly, and to obscure the portrait. The greatest portion of the effects were within a distance of a quarter of an inch, and nearly all of them within a half-inch.

So, to precipitate a portrait and erase it, it was but necessary for the two psychics at each side to move slowly - very slowly indeed - the rear canvas forward and backward with the most steady and slightest motion possible. This was done easily with the fingers through the slit in the soft side curtains; and were any one to violate all rules and "grab" he would only find a portrait "just about finished by the spirits." An ideal scheme, just as mediums would use!

This principle, then, would account for the materializing and dematerializing of the portrait at will; but it necessitated a substitution early in the sitting, just as most magic tricks require. Now the mediums undoubtedly use various means for making the substitution, varying them to suit the occasion. But I think that in most cases they have the finished portrait in the room all of the time. It could be left standing on the far side of the table from where the sitter enters the room, and could be leaned with its face against the wall, or more probably facing into the room. If the soft black curtains reach the floor, one of them can cover the portrait completely so that, should the sitter happen to get in a position to look on that side of the table, he could see nothing. In this case, one of the mediums would take the two chosen canvases and carry them over to that side of the table, and stand them on the floor in front of the portrait. Now, while the other medium seats the sitter at the end of the table in front of the window, the first one has but to lift it into position on the table, the front blank and the rear canvas with portrait, leaving the discarded blank on the floor to be used for the cover of the canvas later. I think this method, being the simplest, is oftenest used; but more complicated means may be employed at times. For instance, the medium who carries out the discarded blanks may bring the portrait back unobserved when she re-enters. Here is how I would do it if I were a lady medium. I should wear a skirt that was really open in front but lapped over in a fold; and I should suspend the portrait on a hanger between my legs under my skirt. If I were quite large I could carry a good-sized portrait here unobserved by all. Of course it would not have to be in this particular position, and in fact could be hung on the outside of the skirt, if the medium keeps that side away from the sitters. But under the skirt would be much safer; and I have always found that female mediums do not hesitate to take advantage of their sex and the sacredness of their skirts, to cover detection.

Many of the Bangs portraits were approximately a standard 20 x 30, and there are also the stunning full length portraits, say, of Queen Victoria, which was 60 x 40 and will be shown in Chapter 3. I am trying to imagine either May or Lizzie Bangs slyly walking across the floor of the séance room, with the sitters in view no less, and having a portrait hung on a hanger under their dress or, better yet, a full size canvas hanging off the side of their dress, and trying not to look suspicious. There is certainly no limit to a magician's imagination.

Abbott:

The sitter naturally thinks that his two chosen blanks are now in the window, and he seems to be seeing right through them and they appear white and clear. He does not dream that his portrait, all finished, is already in the window behind the front canvas, but merely moved back out of focus.

The psychics have previously watched with sharpest eyes for any markings of canvases, and the one bringing in the portraits has a chance when out of the room to duplicate the markings. Or, if the portrait be already in the room, the one medium must divert the sitter's attention by a slate test or otherwise, until the other medium gets the portrait marked. As to the sitter buying his own canvas, as is often reported, it is remarkable that the ones bought correspond exactly with the ones furnished by the mediums, even to the number of threads per inch in the cloth and the thickness of same, etc. Queer isn't it? Dr. Wilmar had the canvases of two thoroughly examined in this manner. One was supplied by the psychics and the other sitter claimed to have bought down town; but they corresponded as above described.

Quote:

The changes of color are, however, to a certain extent *imagination*; and this occurs easily among so many confusing details all coming at the same time. The hair ornament can be made to appear by skilfully pulling off a patch on the back of the portrait which has been stuck on with wax and with a thread attached, but I hardly think it necessary. The choice is undoubtedly "forced" by *suggestion*.

- DAVID P. ABBOTT

Abbott:

The sitter will see the portrait move, and construe it to be a slight narrowing, for the vision being at the time concentrated on the point in question, will see only its movement. The same will apply to the lines of the nose or mouth. Also, at any time, a slightly tighter crowding of the canvases so as to make any feature come out brighter and clearer, coupled with suggestion, will carry the effect of an alteration of the portrait in response to the sitter's request. All of this is the real art of the performance, and what makes it so "strong." It is not what you do, but how you do it. The strong way this has been dressed up and presented to believers, is the secret of the marvel and has made it what it is. The principle alone was not so much, but embellished with this incomparable art of presentation, it has been one of the wonders of the world.

The readers can see how adroit these psychics are at the art of suggestion. Of course every one could not put this act on in so "strong" a manner; but ladies with plenty of "nerve" and years of experience and practice, coupled with a natural aptitude for such work, can do so. It must be remembered that suspicious persons get no portrait. Witness Carrington who was sent by Dr. Funk, and who tried for hours with no success.

Hereward Carrington:

As to the portraits, I can unfortunately say nothing of a conclusive character, since I obtained no picture whatever. We sat for this picture on Saturday, 26th, June, from 1.30 to 4.00 p.m., and from 4.30 to 5.20 p.m., and from 5.30 to 7.10 p.m., without the slightest trace of a picture becoming manifest!

I admit it would have been difficult for me to explain the results by fraud if any portrait appeared on the canvas, but none came. Still, in view of the fraud practiced at the slate-writing sitting, I think that fraud is in all probability the correct explanation of the portrait phenomenon also. On this point however, I do not wish to dogmatize - never having seen a portrait produced - and I leave that part of their mediumship untouched.

I might perhaps say that I bought and brought with me one of the canvases upon which the "spirit portrait" was to appear. A most minute examination of this canvas has failed to detect any preparation, chemical or otherwise. At the present time I feel assured that, if I obtained a sitting with the Misses Bangs, I should be enabled to see the method of the production of the portraits.

I believe that Carrington, who was a prolific writer on psychic subjects such as *The Physical Phenomena of Spiritualism*, 1907, *Death, its Causes and Phenomena*, 1911, and *Psychical Phenomena and the War*, 1918, to name a few, was certainly intent on believing in the reality of mediumistic phenomena but stayed on the fence intellectually and philosophically for a time until, it was said, the medium Mrs. Eileen Garrett, after extensive testing by the American Psychical Institute in 1933, convinced him of the reality of as he said, "mental entities" independent of the control of the medium. This was long after the passing of the Bangs Sisters, so I wonder if his attitude would have been different if he had had these beliefs before he had sat with the Bangs Sisters? He could have kept a healthy skepticism and approached the situation with a fair, open minded attitude, and received positive results I am sure.

Quote:

For myself, I am confident that I have given the correct solution of this mystery; *and although I have never seen the work personally*, I could hardly be more certain of anything than I have solved this mystery in its principal details. The mode of substitution may be different, but substitution it is, and that is certain.

~ DAVID P. ABBOTT

W. USBORNE MOORE AND HEREWARD CARRINGTON

On behalf of Dr. Isaac K Funk, who had investigated the Bangs several times himself and had a high opinion of their powers, Hereward Carrington went to Chicago in 1909 and, as narrated in his book *Personal Experiences in Spiritualism* found, what he considered, fraud, while having a slate writing sitting.

– MOORE

Admiral Moore - Quoting from *Glimpses of the Next State*:

In the body of this book I have alluded to the unworthy methods of anti-Spiritists who profess to tell the public "how the thing is done," and to account for the happenings by normal means. I propose here to give a brief account of a concrete instance of this kind.

After I had seen Dr. I. K. Funk in March, 1909, when we had a conversation about the phenomena that happen in the presence of the Bangs Sisters, he paid the expenses of a conjurer, Mr. Hereward Carrington, to visit Chicago, requesting him to see the Bangs Sisters and report to him the phenomena that he obtained in their presence. Dr. Funk had investigated these mediums several times himself; as will be seen below, he had formed a high opinion of their genuine mediumship. In writing to the mediums to make an appointment he gave no name, as he supposed Mr. Carrington would sit incognito.

Mr. Carrington did go to Chicago and other places about his business, and eventually sent in a report to Dr. Funk of a negative character. It was put on one side of no value.

I believe that Mr. Carrington was unaware that I had investigated the Bangs Sisters in January and March, 1909; and until my report of 1911 was published in *Light*, he was ignorant that I had paid a second series of visits in January of this year.

I have never met Mr. Carrington, and have no animosity against him. I am simply relating facts and commenting upon his obscure proceedings as related by himself in the *Annals of Psychical Science,*

July-September, 1910, an English journal for which he is the agent in America.

After waiting one year and a quarter after his investigation, Mr. Carrington published a long article in the above journal, accusing the Bangs Sisters of fraud. I do not know if this article was verbatim the same as his report to Dr. Funk, but the latter did not see it until April, 1911 and disapproved of its publication.

As it was published in an English journal, the Bangs Sisters knew nothing of this scurrilous production; I was the first to inform them of it in January, 1911. The plan of the room given in the article is wrong; the window and doors are in the wrong place; the table is the wrong size, and put in a place where it has never stood; but, if placed elsewhere, it would not agree with the text of the article. One door is drawn on the plan where there is, in reality, a fixed washstand. There is no furniture in the room, according to the plan; the fact is, it is full of furniture.

In his article, Mr. Carrington says he gave false names. This (if ever was there) would ensure either bad results or none at all. At first, I thought this might be the explanation; but I had to drop this theory for one less flattering to the writer.

The false plan suggests that he has never been inside the house at all; and this explanation is supported by the Bangs Sisters, and by the fact of his inability to correct the mistakes in the correspondence below.

I am bound to say that I hesitate to state positively that a man, hitherto considered honest by those who have associated with him, could be guilty of writing a report of a séance when he had never been inside the house; but we must not forget that he had to send a report of some sort to Dr. Funk, who had paid for his trip.

Hereward Carrington
Response published in *Light*, May 13, 1911
The Bangs Sisters and Fraud

Sir,

In psychic investigation one is truly "between the devil and the deep sea"! If one believes in and champions a medium, as I did in the case of Eusapia Palladino,[15] one is either a "poor observer" or "in league with the medium." On the other hand, if one discovers fraud, one is equally at fault - a villainous "medium hunter" who is not honest in his findings. Surely, one is sailing between Scylla and Charybdis here - and far worse!

I feel I must reply as brief as possible to Vice Admiral W. Usborne Moore's articles in recent issues of *Light*, to which Dr. Funk has called my attention. If I am at fault for not sending a copy of my report to the Bangs Sisters, surely Admiral Moore is equally at fault for not sending me a copy of his criticism; for I do not always see *Light*. As a matter of fact, however, I regard it as nonsense to send a copy of a report to every medium exposed.

I could go through Admiral Moore's reports, if I chose to do so, and point out exactly where, in my opinion, the fraud crept in, in his slate-writing sittings; but it is hardly necessary. I do not consider them genuine, and Admiral Moore does.

As to my being in Chicago at the time, Admiral Moore's doubts as to this are most curious. Perhaps Dr. Funk would confirm this fact; or Mrs. Francis - the widow of the late John R. Francis - editor of *The Progressive Thinker*, on whom I called.

In the Appendices is the Addendum added to Glimpses of the Next State in which Admiral Moore admits that the facts proved that Hereward Carrington was at the house of the Bangs Sisters & also the infamous letter from "Jane Thompson" to Mr. Carrington. Carrington,

---

[15] Eusapia Paladino (1854-1918.) The first physical medium who, according to Nandor Fodor, "stood in the crossfire of collective scientific investigation for more than twenty years all over Europe and America."

continuing his letter in *Light* regarding the precipitated spirit portraits said, "Finally, I wish to say this: if this portrait phenomena can, under virtually the same conditions, be duplicated by fraud, then, surely, its evidential value vanishes. If it could be shown that phenomena, precisely similar to Eusapia's, could be produced by trickery, hitherto unsuspected, then I should give up my belief in her at once...but in the case of the Bangs Sisters it is a little different. For years these spirit portraits were the wonder and envy of all the conjurers and mediums in America. Attempts were made to duplicate their work without success. I myself was "on the fence" regarding their portraits, and so stated in my report. After I had my sittings, Mr. David P. Abbott and myself worked together over this problem; but I was forced to stop at the time, owing to press of other matters, and Mr. Abbott continued his experiments alone. I think I am safe to say that he has now succeeded in duplicating the Bangs Sister's portraits exactly - and by trickery. No chemicals are used, no solar photography, no spraying - nothing of the kind. Two canvases are selected, marked, and placed upon a light easel, which is examined. A bright arc lamp is placed behind the canvases. Investigators may walk around the canvas during the entire process. They may look above, below, behind, on all sides. A picture slowly forms on the inside - between the two canvases - which picture has the same finish and texture as the Bangs' portraits. It can be made to appear slowly, the eyes to open at will, etc., exactly as their pictures do.

The process is, in fact, from all external indications, identical in appearance. In view of this fact, I think the authenticity of the Bangs' "spirit portraits" may seriously be called into question! As to their slate-writing, I am certain I could duplicate it myself, under the same conditions.

- Yours, etc., Hereward Carrington

Vice Admiral Moore:

Sir, I beg to forward to you a letter I have just received from the well-known author and psychic investigator, Rev. I. K. Funk, D. D. There is no doubt Dr. Funk did ask Mr. Carrington to visit the Bangs Sisters. The question is, "Did he ever enter the house?" The Bangs Sisters deny that he did. Lizzie assured me most positively that she would have recognized him, and that they have never sat for him at any time.

What Dr. Funk calls slate-writing is the phenomenon of spirit-writing within a sealed envelopes put between hinged slates, not the "slate writing" we are accustomed to hear of through Eglington, Keeler, the Campbell's, etc.

The following is Dr. Funk's letter:

My Dear Admiral,

Yours to hand in reference to the article by Mr. Carrington, in *The Annals of Psychical Science*, concerning the Bangs Sisters. I made a number of tests of the mediumship of these sisters, both as to picture-painting and slate-writing. I cheerfully bear testimony that I have not had to do with any other mediums who have been able to give me invariably so satisfactory results. In not a single case have I detected fraud, although before my first visit to them I had read carefully the exposé by Dr. Krebs, which was furnished to me by Dr. Hodgson. They certainly did not attempt upon me any of the frauds described by Dr. Krebs, nor did they any of the tricks spoken of by Mr. Carrington. Having been forewarned against them, I would have been an unusually stupid investigator had I been caught by them.

It has been my custom in making investigations, especially when I was not able to explain results, to induce others whom I believed to be keen investigators to make trial, and I would often indicate the particular tests for them to make. I asked Mr. Carrington to visit the Misses Bangs and make certain investigations, as I asked you and others. I never asked anyone to visit a medium under a false name, for I have long believed that fraud begets fraud in these investigations. When I have completed my investigations with these remarkable mediums, I shall gladly publish the exact results.

You are at liberty to make any use of this letter that you think fit.

Yours most respectfully, (signed) I. K. Funk New York, April 18, 1911

Admiral Moore:

Speaking of Mr. Francis, whom Mr. Carrington had mentioned in his letter:

He mentions Mr. Francis. I have a letter from that gentleman dated, September 16, 1909 (three months after the visit of Mr. Carrington to Chicago), in which he says: "I wish to say to you in all candor that *I believe that their* (the Bangs Sisters), *spirit paintings are genuine productions* originating from the spirit world." The italics are those of Mr. Francis. I will deposit the letter with you if you desire.

The last two paragraphs of Mr. Carrington's letter contain another "red herring." The Abbott-Marriott trick is well known in England. I have seen it often, and it surpasses in skill almost every conjuring trick I have ever witnessed. When my friends ask me how the Bangs pictures *appear* to come, I say: "Go and see Dr. Wilmar's spirit paintings." But the conditions no more resemble the Bangs Sisters' conditions than a locomotive boiler resembles a teapot. The operator must have a heavy easel, and the picture comes on the wrong canvas. The method is known to me, and was known to me before I met Dr. Wilmar. It was found out by an exhibition of my own models, and by one of our best trance mediums (whose modesty prevents me naming him), about the time it was discovered by Mr. David Abbott.

I respect Mr. Abbott. He candidly owns that all his theories about the Bangs Sisters' pictures previous to 1909 were entirely erroneous. I ask myself this plain question: Why has not this diligent conjurer been to sit with the Bangs Sisters? He lives within a reasonable distance. If he does sit with them, he will find his latest theory as rotten as his previous one.

In conclusion, I have only to say that the Bangs Sisters do not sit for "slate-writing," and that no psychic in the United States I have met cares a button whether Mr. Hereward Carrington believes in him or not. He has no influence, and cannot forward the tenets of spiritism by a hair's breadth.

I have not done yet with this S. P. R. expert, but my letter is, I fear, already too long; I can wait.

Harassment & Vindication
A Card from the Bangs Sisters
Chicago, June 9, 1891

A few months ago when a cowardly raid was made on us at one of our parlor séances at our own home in this city, a number of sensational articles appeared in the columns of the press to the great detriment of our reputation. We then requested the public to withhold judgement until a court of justice had thoroughly investigated the matter. The Grand Jury of Cook County, after having heard the statements of the witnesses for the state and discharged us, although not a single one of our witnesses for the state was or could be heard by them, thus deciding after hearing the testimony of our prosecutors, and without a single word of defense, that the charges were baseless.

The object of this card, which we ask a generous press to circulate as freely as it did the articles to our injury, is to inform the public of the final results of this effort to degrade and humiliate us.

- BANGS SISTERS

On April 2, 1888, there was published a "spectacular arrest" in one of the more prejudiced publications in Chicago. Two plainclothes detectives raided an actual séance of the Bangs and according to them, or whomever, seized a "ghostly Russian princess" in a regal gown and the spirit resisted furiously, throwing punches madly. One of the detectives then supposedly shouted, "I have a warrant for you, May Bangs," and, they also said, the princess mask that she was wearing, fell off, revealing it to be her. The sisters and their male attendants put up such a fight that the police, said the press, "finally drew their guns to clear the room."

The Washington Post then printed that a search of the house revealed a satchel of white muslin shrouds and the like, sets of whiskers of various hues, wigs and moustaches. The cabinet, satchel, and the sisters, it said, were then loaded into a patrol wagon and taken to the station and locked up. Due to technicalities, they were released.

I am trying to imagine May or Lizzie Bangs wearing a moustache, or "whiskers" tromping around in the dark. In what seems like the same event, *The Chicago Daily Tribune* published in March, 1890, that a Grand Jury failed 'due to technicalities' to indict the Bangs Sisters.

I have always believed that it takes more than one report, or one individual to establish a solid, prosecutorial case in any form of jurisprudence. By one report, it goes against reason to assume that the Bangs Sisters, early on, attempted fraud by impersonating spirits, etc., but that is not saying that it is not true. Perhaps it did happen, but it is not enough to convict them, especially when we have other reports—seemingly concerning the same incident—stating that they were not guilty as decided by a Grand Jury. The jurists report, in my opinion, holds more weight when compared with the jaundiced report of detectives bursting in to the Bang's house.

CHAPTER 3

THE SPIRIT PRECIPITATED PORTRAITS OF THE BANGS SISTERS

―――――――→ঽ❂ৼ←――――――

"It seemed like a rainstorm on the canvas, the colors seemingly being pelted on in waves"

~ EYEWITNESS ACCOUNT TOLD TO C.F. ELDREDGE

Sworn Affidavit:
Chesterfield, Indiana
August 21, 1909
State of Indiana, Madison S.S.

Tom O'Neal, President of the Indiana Association of Spiritualists; James Millspaugh, Vice President of said association; Lydia Jessup, Secretary of said association, and Rebecca McKee, J. M. Walker, S. L. Louiso and Lewis Johnson, Trustee of said association, being duly sworn, upon their oath depose and say: that on the 20th day of August, 1909, they were present at a séance held by the Bangs Sisters under test conditions, for these affiants above to receive a portrait of some former member of said association, deceased, which portrait is to become the property of said association, to be hung in the auditorium; that the affiants witnessed the development of said portrait, which they recognize as the portrait of Alex P. Mckee, a former member and Treasurer of said association; that said picture was developed on canvas, or stretcher on a frame, which stretcher and frame were selected by one of these affiants from an assortment of such articles, all similar in form and appearance, without any suggestion or indication from the said Bangs Sisters; that said portrait developed on said canvas or stretcher in a period of eight minutes within the full view of all these affiants, in daylight; and affiants further say that they are firmly convinced that said portrait was so developed by spirit powers solely, and that no human, earthly agency contributed to the development of said portrait. The said affiants recognize in said portrait the exact likeness of the said Alex P. McKee.

Subscribed and sworn to before me, on this 21ˢᵗ day of August, 1909

WILLIAM ROWLAND, NOTARY PUBLIC
MY COMMISSION EXPIRES MARCH 15, 1913
(ALL AFFIANTS MENTIONED ABOVE, SIGNED THEIR NAMES)

The Sunflower
April 15, 1905
Spirit Portraits

I was glad when I read the last article in my last paper defending the Bangs Sisters that I gave a good old fashioned shout. God bless the *Sunflower* for defending good and true mediumship, and God help them to put down all frauds.

I am the proud possessor of two spirit portraits, one of my son and one of my daughter, procured through the wonderful gift of spirit power, by the Bangs Sisters. I never had a photograph taken of either, so no one could say they were copied. My son's portrait was finished in just seven minutes by my watch, and my daughter's in eighteen, no earthly hand touching the canvas. I sat in front of the table on which the canvas rested, and my eyes were on guard every moment.

Knowing the facts I cannot sit patiently and hear the Bangs Sisters so cruelly slandered. I am ready anytime to face a regiment in defense of them. I know what I know, and am willing the whole world shall know that my portraits are perfect and a great comfort to my husband and myself; and there is not gold enough on this earth to buy them.

Yours for defense of all good mediums,
Mrs. Harriet Duhl, 313 Columbia Street, Elmira, New York

The National Spiritualist
July 1, 1940
Transcendence in Oil
(The Bangs Sisters)

In the soft light of a homey little living room on Chicago's West Side, two men and two women sat gathered about a plain oak table standing close to a window facing an open court. The time was the late fall in 1894. A 20 by 24 inch frame enclosing a piece canvas such as is commonly used by artists, lay on top of the table; one edge of the frame resting against the inner sill of the window held the frame and canvas in an inclined position. The window was so shaded over the top and sides as to allow the sunlight to flood directly through the canvas.

Sitting as close as possible to the table, the men faced the canvas. Facing each other on opposite sides of the table sat the two ladies, each holding the upper corners of the frame with a hand. Their heads bowed, the long lashes of their closed eyes brushing their cheeks, they sat in studied concentration.

Suddenly the men facing the canvas leaned forward in their chairs and sat upright, their eyes wide and fixed on the canvas, from which a thin, vapor-like transparent mist was rising. Unmistakable, almost unbelievable and indefinable, they watched the phenomenon take form.

Beauty and mystery had entered the room. The sunlight pouring through the canvas was replaced by sweeping color and the *supposedly dead* took form and held the watchers spellbound.

"Impossible!"

Nevertheless, somewhere, perhaps obscured by the ethereal mists hovering over the canvas, spirit artists were at work reproducing a conjured likeness of the long departed father of a famous county attorney.

The two men, an attorney and financier and a lumber magnate, who had watched the transformation take place, stared at each other in amazement. It was the attorney who had procured the canvas, brought it to the séance room, fastened it in the frame and then placed it in position. The strong light flooding through the window made deception unthinkable. All present were not only able to see the light of day through the canvas, but could also see behind and all around it.

In quiet patience the ladies sat through the séance, their hands never moving from the corners of the frame, while the colors poured over, then merged into a complete and lifelike life-sized portrait of the attorney's departed father.

Illusion? Deception of some sort? Not possible, though that was exactly what the agnostic and very skeptical attorney and his friend were expecting.

The astonished men took the portrait from the table and scrutinized it closely. Their comments were generally favorable, but the attorney said that, while his father had worn a full beard in his maturity, he later had it trimmed to a goatee, which he considered more becoming of an older man.

On hearing this the sisters begged to be permitted to try again in hope that the spirits would make the change from beard to goatee. Upon his consenting, the portrait was returned to the table, and once again the two ladies and the men took up their respective places for another visitation of the spirit artists.

What followed surely was enough to persuade even the most skeptical of the truth of the powers possessed by these two Chicago ladies.

It was a moment of deep, charged silence. Scarcely visible on the electrified atmosphere, a waft of transparent blue mist hovered over the table. Slowly the colors on the canvas began to fade until at last the canvas was as absolutely blank as when first brought in the séance room. There was no further change for a few moments. Then the sun again pouring through the canvas. Once more the rising mists and falling shadows. And again the two friends leaned forward in their chairs, fascinated by the phenomenon too great almost for mortal comprehension.

Slowly the portrait of the father took form on the canvas. It was the same strong face of a man in his prime, but this time the face wore a goatee!

The father had left the world leaving no photograph or portrait behind that could convey his likeness to anyone who had not known him in life. This fact, plus the two sittings, make the achievement startling indeed.

This next item is an example of an early sitting with only one of the Bangs Sisters and the portrait was precipitated under a table and took quite a long time to complete. I copied it word for word from the original hand written letter. No photograph existed of the spirit that precipitated:

The Bangs Sisters
Will C .Hodge
October, 1898
Light of Truth
Instrumentality of May and Lizzie Bangs, 3 Elizabeth Street, Chicago, IL.

The new development which has come to them within the past twelve months, the producing of portraits of our departed friends, is at once beautiful, grand and inspiring.

Arrangements were made to secure a portrait of my wife who had passed to the land of spirits several years ago, and of whom I had no likeness whatsoever. A perfectly clean canvas 25 x 30 was stretched on a frame and placed by myself under a common table, around which a heavy curtain was drawn for the purpose of excluding the light. I wrote my name, the date, and other private marks upon the canvas for identification, and patiently awaited results. After three and a half hours, the guides signified that the forces were getting exhausted, and another sitting would be necessary to complete the work, and added, "You cannot look at the picture." Taking the canvases from under the table there appeared two faces, one unmistakably my wife, the other a representation of a Sicilian girl, Lily, who often entertained my wife when in mortal form.

These were all incompleteness of detail which I was told would be remedied at another sitting. At the second sitting, which also required three and one half hours, another face was added to the canvas - that of a spirit known to me by the name of Pearl, who has been my family's servant for more than 20 years.

Upon removing the canvas the second time there was a finish of completeness of detail truly wonderful. No brushes, paint, or coloring matter of any description was furnished. The only requirement being the presence of one of the mediums and patience on the part of myself.

This next piece is an undated, unsigned early hand written letter describing a portrait sitting using an actual pot of paint for the spirit artists to use, and one hand used by the medium, the other linked with the sitters. It was probably circa. 1895-96.

A canvas was placed in front of a window on a frame or easel and the light from around the canvas blocked out with a frame of black cloth. On a table in front of the canvas was a small table with a pot of paint upon it. The medium was a mixture of various colors of paint suitable for oil work on canvas. On one side May; in front of the canvas sat the subjects for whom the picture was to be painted. All three joined hands and the free hand of the Bangs sister grasped the frame of the painting.

Soon the picture began to appear on the canvas as if it came from the rear. There was no visual evidence that the paint was on its way to the picture. After it was done there was no decrease in the amount of paint. The paintings took from 35 minutes to an hour and a half to complete.

Vice Admiral W. Usborne Moore
January 20th, 1909
Portrait of Iola

Atmospheric conditions good...Went to the Bangs Sisters for a profile portrait of Iola, as arranged on the 18th. Everything was ready at 10.50, and we sat till 11.30. I had in my dollar-pocket a *carte-de-visite* of Iola, taken in the year 1874. The mediums had never seen this or any other photograph in my possession. Fifteen minutes after we sat in the window the face and bust appeared; the profile was looking to the right, precisely the same aspect as it has now, framed, hanging in my room.

Remember, I was looking through the back of the picture, and it was forming on the further side of that one of the two canvases nearer to me; consequently, had it gone on as it was and been finished, it would now (when framed) be profile left. When the portrait was nearly finished the two canvases were lowered towards me on to the table (the mediums being impressed, apparently, to do this). A telegraphic message came by taps to May Bangs, who said: "She wants this picture for your wife specially, as well as for you. She thinks that your wife would prefer to see her in the pose to which she is accustomed." Up went the canvases again to the window, and I found that the whole picture was changed round, so that the profile looked to the left instead of to the right. In a few minutes the portrait was completed, May Bangs remarking: "She says she cannot put in the hand."

From the time the face and bust first appeared to the time the canvases were separated and the finished picture put on the sofa in the next room, twenty-five minutes elapsed. Neither of the psychics had ever seen the *carte-de-visite* in my pocket. How did they know normally that there ought to be any hand in the picture? As a matter of fact, in this photo there is a hand (the left) supporting the cheek on its left side. This was omitted in the colored picture.

When the portrait was finished, it bore a very close resemblance to the photograph. It was looking in the same direction - to the right. As to likeness, it is impossible for anyone who compares the photograph with the picture to deny that they are one and the same individual. At the same time the picture is by no means a slavish copy of the photograph. Its pose is more upright, the face spirituelle, and the dress not exactly the same. There is a firmness, a decision, and an appearance of calm and contented happiness in the face which is absent in the *carte-de-visite*. It is a work of art. I can only say this of one other picture in my collection. They are all interesting, and each has its peculiar test value; but some of the dresses are stiff, and there are many anatomical deficiencies. This one, however, is without a flaw, and there is just sufficient difference between it and the photograph to show distinctly to the most casual observer that one is not a professional copy of the other.

By this time the Bangs Sisters and I were, more or less, on the terms of fellow students, and they offered to give me any test I desired. It was arranged that in future I should bring my own slates, rubber bands, and ink.

Admiral Moore
January 22, 1909
Portrait of Cleopatra

Atmospheric conditions were bad; it was raining outside, and the air was heavy and close. Sat with the Bangs Sisters for a picture of Cleopatra. As before, two canvases were produced, covered with blank drawing paper, laid face to face, and held up against a window, the bottom of the canvases, in this case, resting on the sill of the window, as they were much larger in size than those used for the two portraits of Iola already obtained. I sat between the two psychics, as on previous occasions, my eyes looking straight into the center of the canvases from a distance of two feet to two feet six inches. We took our places at 10.55. About 11.05 the form began to appear, and it was roughly finished in ten minutes. We were then directed, by taps on a slate, to put the canvases on the table and sit around it. We moved the table to the center of the room, placed the canvases flat upon it, covered them over with the felt table cloth, and sat around as directed. At 11.30 we were informed that the picture could be raised; the canvases were now separated and the picture put on a sofa in a neighboring drawing-room.

In all precipitations through the mediumship of the Bangs Sisters the picture is found to be on the further side of the canvas which is next to the sitter. The stuff of which the picture is composed is damp, and rubs off at the slightest touch, like soot. Notwithstanding this, the paper on the canvas furthest from the sitter is unsoiled. The picture, while in progress, can be seen clearly through the back of the canvas; but of course it presents the reverse aspect to that when it is framed - left arm for the right, and so forth. The portrait of Cleopatra is practically the same now as it was when it was lifted from the table. Afterwards, but not while I was looking at it, the colours deepened a little, flowers were added to the embroidery of the dress, a ring was put on the finger of the left hand, and the picture acquired a general appearance of greater richness and finish. It was hanging in the lecture-room of the London Spiritualist Alliance for four months, and it is therefore unnecessary to describe it. It cannot be called a work of high art; the dress is stiff, and the anatomical features are deficient; but it is undoubtedly a representation of an Egyptian queen, and, considering the way in which it was done, a fine example of spirit power.

January 29, 1911
Portrait of Iola

Admiral Moore's guide's father and his father briefly appear on the canvas before Iola appears. In this sitting, Admiral Moore was also pinching the canvases together as an experiment.

I arrived with my two canvases a little before 4.00 p.m., and we assembled for the séance at 4.15. I put the canvases up as before, and asked Lizzie Bangs to pinch them together on her side, while I did the same on mine. May Bangs sat opposite the canvases, in the visitor's chair, as on the previous occasion. The doors were thrown open, and the sealing of the window examined. Soon after the canvases were set up, the one next to us began mottling on the inside, as it did the day before. This time, not only did the face of my guide's father appear for a short time, but that of my father. May Bangs, as before, left her seat several times and moved about the house. She appeared to be absolutely unable to sit still.

About 5.00 p. m., we were told that we were "too intent" and that we were to get up from our chairs and move about the house to "change vibrations." I did not leave the room, and never lost sight of the canvases; between 5.05 and 5.55 p.m., I smoked a cigar, sitting at first in the visitor's chair, two and a half-feet from the canvases. Lizzie Bangs came to her seat about 5.20, and I resumed mine, both of us pinching the canvases. At about 5.45 May Bangs was sent for to take her proper seat, and I took the visitor's seat. Even then she could not keep still.

Some of the delay was owing to a blunder of mine. It had been arranged at Detroit that Iola was to put round her neck a chain with a locket, and that I was to put my watch on the table close to the canvases, in order that the invisible artists might extract the gold from it. This I had done the previous day; but today, 5.30, it suddenly occurred to me that I had forgotten about my watch. I then put it down on the table.

The changes in the canvas first showed by a rose tinted light at the bottom, after the faces had appeared on the white mottling. About 5.15 p.m., a black patch appeared right in the middle of the canvas, and increased in size and darkness. This is then opposite to what usually happens in the precipitations under ordinary circumstances - the dark shade begins at the edges of the canvas. Lizzie Bangs and I watched this black shade growing till 6.00 p.m., when it was dark outside, and we were told to light the room up. To my dismay, the canvas appeared blank. We asked: "Shall we light the globe?" (A "wandering lead.") Answer: "Not yet."

A few minutes later the message came to "hang the globe behind the canvases." I did this myself. We were soon, all three in our places. I was told to take up my watch with one hand, and pinch the canvases with the other. At 6.05 the picture began. The face and form were finished, as they are now, by 6.20; but there was a smudge on the neck, and the top of the canvas was very badly rubbed. The background was unfinished. I remarked on this. The message came: "Cover the picture, put out the lights, and come back later." We covered the picture, put out the lights, and all went downstairs to tea, after I had examined my labels on the window sashes. In an hour we returned, switched on the lights, uncovered the picture, and found the defects entirely removed; the background was evidently improved but not finished. I was told to take away the picture, and the background would be finished in the hotel, or the passage home; it would be "mottled." I departed with both the canvases under my arm. The next time I saw the picture I was in London, on March 9, and found that the background was mottled.

A gramophone played while the sitting was going on. Mrs. Bangs and two dogs strayed in and out of the room. On both days everything was of the most casual description. The messages came sometimes by impression through one of the sisters, but more often by taps on a slate. I obtained good evidence that all these messages were true communications from the "other side."

As I was leaving the house, in order to coax the sisters into a genial frame of mind for the letter test which was to take place the following morning, I put into their hands a pamphlet issued by the Society for Psychical Research, London, in January, 1901, describing them as cheats and imposters of the first order. I never did believe this account; and, after hearing the evidence of a certain gentleman in Chicago who knew the writer well, I am now certain the whole story is the outcome of the latter's excited imagination.

Two Rough Farmers
March, 1909

Admiral Moore, who had had a slate writing sitting in the early part of the day, was commenting on May Bangs' nervous energy during the experience, and went on to say:

The nervousness and want of self-control of May Bangs on this occasion, when a fine manifestation was partially spoilt, may be accounted for by an incident that took place late in the afternoon, and which must have taxed the mediumistic powers of the two sisters to the utmost. Two farmers from Oregon had come to the house between four and five o'clock. One brought a photograph with him into the room in his pocket, and asked that a portrait of his deceased wife might be precipitated. The other accompanied him to the sitting, as a friend, intending to ask for a precipitated portrait of his deceased wife if that of his companion should prove to be a success; he left his photograph in his overcoat pocket, in the hall. Two canvases were produced, and the sitting commenced. In a short time the face and bust of a woman appeared. They were those of an apparently refined person, with delicate dress and etherealized countenance. The man watched it with undisguised impatience, and, when it was nearly finished, exclaimed: "That's not my wife; if I take that picture home,

99

my daughters will say that is not their mother!" Immediately the picture faded away. Two more canvases were set up, and *another* face and bust in due time appeared. After watching their development for some ten minutes, the man said to his friend (who, remember, had not disclosed his intention of asking for a precipitation): "Bill, that's not my wife; that's your wife!" "I could have told you that some time ago," was his reply. The development went on till this portrait was finished to the complete satisfaction of the husband, and the picture was laid on one side on a chair. "Now," said the psychics to the first man, who had been disappointed, "we will try again to obtain for you a precipitation of your wife as she was in earth life." Canvases were set up as before (this time not in the window, for it had become dark), and presently a face and bust of his wife developed, precisely as in the photograph which he had brought into the room. It was now about 6.40 or 6.50, and I came to the house. May Bangs opened the door for me, and begged me to come into the séance room to see what had happened. On going in, I was confronted by the picture of what appeared to me to be a man - a friar. Fortunately, I said nothing to betray my belief in the sex of the person whose portrait was before me. I had a short conversation with the two men. Both were highly pleased at their success in obtaining good portraits of their wives just as they were in earth life. They accepted the pictures, and went away delighted.

It should be noted that the second portrait was taken down from the window to finish.

Article Shows Spirit Picture

There were no paints or brushes in the room, nor the house, for all we knew. We watched the picture come on the canvas, which was finished in less than thirty minutes. It is an exact likeness of our little girl. There never was a picture of her anything like this taken before, and no picture of her was closer to the Bangs Sisters than Decatur. They never saw the child in life, so how could they have produced such an exact likeness of her? I do not say there are no frauds, for we know there are, but we all know that (when) there is a counterfeit, there must be a true one some place.

- MR. CHARLES PECK, 1249 NORTH STREET, DECATUR, ILINOIS

Letter from Dr. Isaac K. Funk
To The Bangs Sisters
Written upon the paper of the
Funk & Wagnall's Company
New York
December 22, 1904

I send you a check covering the balance of the two pictures, including frames, which were completed. As soon as the package comes with the third picture in it I will send you the check for that. I trust that your artist friends were able to get that picture also correct. The one of the old lady whom I called mother Seannette Thompson seemed to be a prefect one. I hope it will please my wife when it arrives. After their arrival I will let several of my friends see them, including Professor Hyslop,[16] and I hope that we may be able to see you both in New York City, and have experiments made that will bring to the knowledge of the public, in a scientific way, the marvels which you seem so able to perform.

Admiral Moore Questions the
Spirit Iola, at a Trumpet Séance with
Mrs. Etta Wriedt
February 4, 1909
Detroit, Michigan, U.S.A.

Question: "Were you present while your portrait was precipitated?"

Answer: "I was there all the time, and the artists were doing the picture for me. There are three artists, one for drawing, one for colours, and one for magnetism."

Question: "Did you mark the profile portrait which has gone home?"

Answer: "Yes, I inscribed it to G."

---

[16] James Hervey Hyslop (1854-1920), Professor of Logic and Ethics from 1889-1902 at Columbia University, New York, and one of the most distinguished American psychical researchers. He wrote several books, including *Science and a Future Life*, 1906; *Borderland of Psychical Research*, 1906; *Life After Death*, 1918, and *Contact with the Other World*, 1919.

Iola also said: "What made the picture a success was your being present. Had you laid your gold watch upon the table, I could have extracted the essence and put a gold pin in my hair or dress. If you had taken roses with you to the séance room, I could have put in roses. Spirits love the flowers."

The spirit controls of the Bangs Sisters would take the essence of any available material, organic or otherwise, and utilize it for the precipitation. They would use the chemical essence from the color of a dress or other clothes, flowers and other plants especially, and minerals such as gold, silver or other substances in the immediate vicinity.

The Sunflower
September 23, 1905
Two Fine Portraits

Hanging on a wall in an upper room of the pleasant home on Sunset Avenue owned and occupied by Hon. and Mrs. Ezra J. Beckwith, are two very fine portraits: one of their daughter, Mrs. Eva J. Conkling, who died some ten years ago. And the other their son, John D. Beckwith, formerly of Little Falls and then later of Utica, who died a little more than two years since. They are really very fine pictures from an artistic point of view and excellent portraits as all those who knew the originals will testify. Apparently they are done in what goes by the name of pastel painting, but nowhere is there about them any trace of the touches by a brush, crayon, a cloth, a pencil or any other instrument. They are in color and but for that in all respects resemble photographs taken by a camera. Both are busts, the pictures being of the usual size of paintings or crayons of that character. The remarkable thing about them and the one most interesting is how they are made and this Mr. Beckwith told interestingly to a press reporter yesterday.

They are what is known as spirit pictures or pictures painted by spirit artists. They were done by the Bangs Sisters, as they call themselves, of Chicago. Mr. Beckwith had seen some of their work and this spring determined to see and investigate for himself.

Accordingly, having business in Chicago, he took Mrs. Beckwith with him and improved the earliest opportunity after his arrival to call at their apartments in the residence part of the city. They had engagements for all the work they could do that day, but made an appointment for Mr. Beckwith at 11 o'clock the next morning and at the hour the Uticans were on hand. They were ushered into the ordinary drawing room or parlor of a dwelling and seated before a table, which was immediately in front of a window, and the proceedings commenced at once. Into the window were put two frames, each containing a canvas as for an oil, pastel or crayon. The picture appeared on the canvas nearest the Uticans. The two artists, one on each side of the frame, simply each put a hand thereon and sat there quietly for a few minutes. The first indication of a change noticeable was a darkening of the edges of the hitherto unmarked canvas. After perhaps ten minutes the outlines of the photograph appeared quickly on the canvas. The face came out plain enough to be recognized and then seemed to disappear and come again, each time a little more plainly. What at first was dim became plain and plainer, and last of all the coloring appeared. Surely no artist could have put it on more naturally or done the tinting with better taste. The Bangs Sisters suggested to Mr. & Mrs. Beckwith that if there were any criticisms to make as the picture was developing, attention be called to it, but only once was the opportunity improved.

The pictures were developed in full view of Mr. & Mrs. Beckwith, who sat so near as to touch the table on the other side of which was the window holding the canvas. The portraits came out from the cloth before their very eyes. A remarkably short space of time was occupied—thirty five minutes for the picture of the son and thirty minutes for that of the daughter. No living artist with brush, crayon, or pastels could have done it better if hours instead of minutes had been employed. They are certainly excellent portraits, true to life. How were they made? That is the most natural question to ask and the one most difficult to answer. Mr. & Mrs. Beckwith had never seen or been seen by the Bangs Sisters till the day before the pictures were made. They made no appointments by mail or wire, nor did anyone in Utica know of their intentions to put these artists to test. There were certainly no collusion or knowledge beforehand of what was intended or expected.

Mr. & Mrs. Beckwith had in their luggage photographs of their children, but these were not taken out or shown to anybody until the pictures were finished and delivered and then in their room they compared the portraits with the photographs and marveled at the likeness. The Bangs Sisters claim the same work can be done as well in any other house as in their own and, when desired, go to the homes of their patrons and the spirit artists do as well there as anywhere. Mr. Beckwith says in no way could the Chicago Ladies have known him, or any member of his family or intention to order pictures. The work is artistically done and the pictures are certainly life like. The Bangs Sisters claim that they were painted by spirit artists. Even the most pronounced skeptic can only guess and wonder, while the faithful latterly believe the statement.

- UTICA DAILY PRESS

I have to wonder how David Abbott and Hereward Carrington, or any other of the outstanding critics of the Bangs Sisters could explain, in conjuring terms, how Mr. Beckwith's portraits came about other than spirit artists?

Quote:

Throughout these many years of public misunderstanding and criticism, the leaders of Spiritualism have been trying to make their followers and the Christian world believe that there is nothing in Spiritualism or its phenomena to detract from the true meaning of the Christian Bible. It is now proper time to call to the attention of the critics of Spiritualism that perhaps knowledge of the real relation of the invisible to the visible can be observed in the phenomena of spirit paintings and in cosmic processes in general, with the change of chemical spectrum brought to the surface.

- Ron Nagy, Author, Lily Dale, Historian

The Published Material
of James Coates, Ph. D., F.A.S.
Photographing the Invisible, 1911
Portraits Painted by Invisible Artists

It is an honor to include the work of James Coates in this Bangs Sisters book. The testimonies he published are worth their weight in gold as regards their importance to upholding the integrity of these great mediums, and it also strengthens the overall truth that the early 20th century provided the positive evidence of life after death and spirit communication, as recorded, through the records of Historic Spiritualism and Physical Mediumship. We are fortunate to have had these individuals who took the time to write down their experiences and we are equally fortunate to the individuals who recorded and published these eyewitness testimonies of the precipitated spirit portraits.

James Coates:

> For years I have heard and read of the mediumship of the Bangs Sisters of Chicago. They are as well-known at Chesterfield, Indiana; Lily Dale, New York; etc., as at Chicago. Consequently they have been tested in the exercise of their mediumship in residences not their own. Although super-normally produced "spirit paintings and portraits" stand apart from psychic photography, I thought, as the agents for their production—intelligent operators in the Invisible— were identical, it might be possible that a little research would reveal a similarity in the laws underlying both the paintings and the photographs. It has. This will be seen in the agreement running through the statements made by the various reputable persons in the centers as wide apart as the United States, Canada, India and Great Britain. For obvious reasons, the greater number of the writers and the attestations are American.

> The Bangs Sisters have been mediums since childhood, but it was not till the autumn of 1894 that they began to get spirit paintings.

> In spirit photography, as many of the processes do not lend themselves to the observation of the sitters, this rare phenomenon of portraits painted by Invisibles is enhanced by the fact that *all the work can be followed, from the purchase of the canvases to the "precipitation of the finished portrait."*

> There are two styles of work. For the more delicate, spiritual and symbolic pictures, the spirit artists furnish their own coloring matter; but for the usual portraiture, colored French pastels are placed in front of the canvas, and these are used by the spirit artists by a process called "precipitation." The effects are harmonious, and the refined blending is truer to nature than if similar portraits were produced by material portrait painters.

2. Bangs in Black, late 1870's, Elizabeth left, May, right

3. Alex Mckee, precipitated in eight minutes in daylight, ibid.
Camp Chesterfield

4. Iola, guide of Admiral Moore, from Glimpses of the Next State by Admiral Usborne Moore

5. Cleopatra, precipitated for Admiral Moore, Courtesy, Portsmouth Spiritualist Church, England

6. William T. Stead, black and white photo of colored portrait, from
Dawn of the Awakened Mind, by John S. King

7. Indian girl Blossom, full length, photo courtesy of The National Spiritualist Association of Churches (NSAC), Lily Dale

8. Dr. Sharp, spirit guide of one of America's most famous direct voice mediums, Etta Wriedt, ibid. Camp Chesterfield

9. Queen Victoria, full length portrait in all her splendor, ibid. Camp Chesterfield, precipitated for Dr. Carson of Kansas City

10. Audrey Alford, black and white photo of color portrait precipitated in 22 minutes at a demonstration in front of a large audience at Camp Chesterfield in 1911, from Photographing the Invisible by James Coates

11. Indian Girl with turquoise necklace,
Courtesy of Wonewoc Spiritualist Camp, Wisconsin

12. Spirit Clara, with the roving eyes,
Courtesy of The Lily Dale Assembly

13. Thomas Skidmore, husband of Marion Skidmore, ibid. NSAC

14. George Mcglean, very early Bangs portrait

15. Mrs. A. B. Caldwell, ibid. NSAC

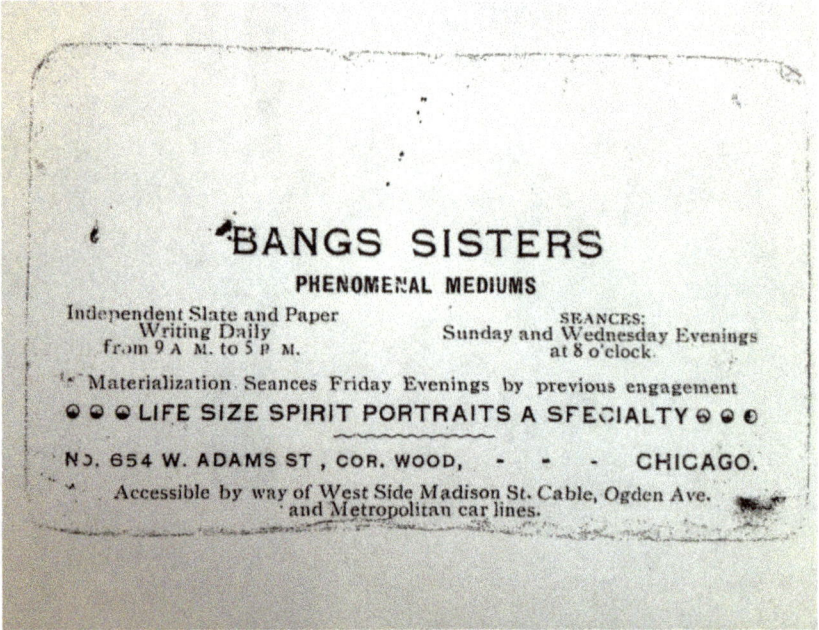

16. Classic Bangs business card, 1909

17. Early shot of Camp Chesterfield, 1910

18. Audrey Alford color photo, after being donated years later to Camp Chesterfield with necklace dematerialized. Courtesy of Camp Chesterfield, Indiana. Mrs. Alford was a cousin of the famous materialization medium, Ethel Post Parrish of Camp Silver Belle, Euphrata, PA.

19. The Hett Memorial Art Gallery, Camp Chesterfield

20. The Hett Memorial Art Gallery, Camp Chesterfield

21. Library Street home of Bangs Sisters, Lily Dale, New York, 1900's, house is still there in present day

22. Early Lily Dale in its classic heyday,
known as The City of Light 1903-06

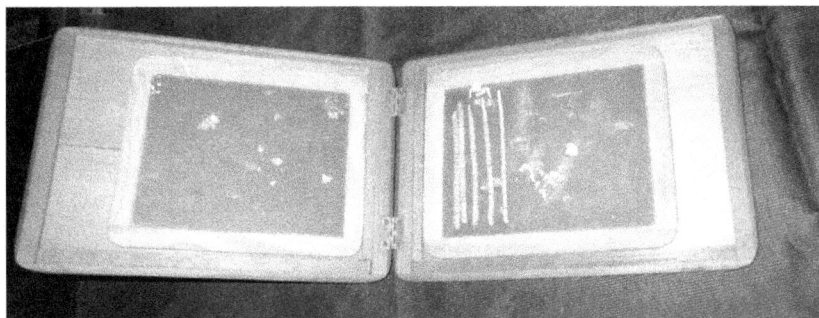

23. Photo of hinged slates, commonly used for independent slate writing,
Courtesy of Lily Dale Musuem, Lily Dale

24. Hypatia, ibid. John S. King

25. Dr. Daughtery and family, ibid. Camp Chesterfield. Dr. Daughtery went to the Bangs Sisters to have a portrait of his deceased wife. When he went to leave after the sitting, the spirit artists had precipitated on to the canvas not only his wife, but himself and his deceased twin daughters. An entire family portrait gift from the spirit artists

26. Spirit World, ibid. Camp Chesterfield. The spirits in the portrait were Mr. and Mrs. Woodmansee, cousins of the sitter Cora Smith, seen crossing the river to their spirit home

27. Thanksgiving at the Bangs Home, Elizabeth and May, sitting fourth and fifth starting clockwise from bottom left

28. Independent writing slates from the book Marguerite Hunter

29. Rare black and white photo of color portrait from spirit dictated book, *The Valley of the Shadow and Beyond,* of Ralph Waldo Emerson.

30. *The Valley of the Shadow and Beyond*, portrait of Dr. J. A. Buchanan

31. *The Valley of the Shadow and Beyond*, portrait of spirit guide, Mary

PROGRAM

MR. P. T. SELBIT

Offering a Wierd and Wonderful European Sensation

SPIRIT PAINTINGS

DR. WILMAR'S RIDDLE OF THE CENTURY.

Famous Paintings Reproduced by Spirit Artists in Full View of the Audience, Upon Ordinary Canvasses Chosen by Themselves.

(Continued on Next Program Page.)

32. Conjurer, Selbit Ad, from The Spirit Portrait Mystery; Its Final Solution, by David P. Abbott

33. Spirit girl, Pat Murphy, ibid. NSAC

34 William Mervin, 37 years old, Wisconsin, ibid. NSAC

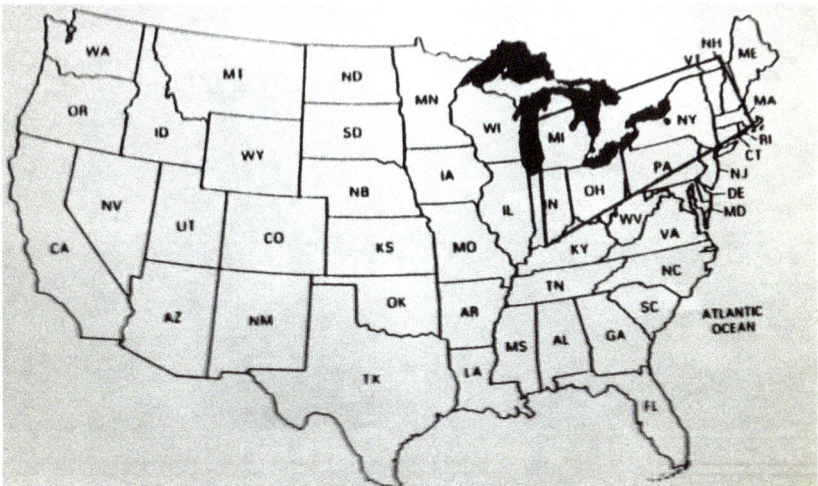

35. The area surrounding the Great Lakes which has produced an
astounding amount of powerful and famous physical mediums

36. Early photo of Bangs Sisters, circa. 1882 Elizabeth, right, May, left

37. Hereward Carrington, British-born, well known American author and investigator

38. Vice Admiral William Usborne Moore, the greatest champion for the Bangs Sisters mediumship.

39. Ella Leach, full size portrait, ibid. James Coates.

40. Poyesh Kanti, ibid. James Coates

41. David P. Abbott, well known author, amateur magician and inventor

42. Edgar Bean, ibid.
Camp Chesterfield

43. Don Keeler, ibid. Camp Chesterfield. This young lad drowned at the camp and later manifested on to the canvas. The portrait was donated to the camp by his father Joseph Keeler

44. Emily Carson, ibid. Camp Chesterfield, precipitated in 1894, first wife of Dr. Carson, Kansas City

45. Young girl, Dorothy Robinson, Courtesy of Morris Pratt Institute, Wisconsin

46. Young man wearing cameo, Courtesy of Morris Pratt Institute, Wisconsin

47. Fred Cropsey, ibid., Through the Valley of The Shadow and Beyond

48. The Great Oleson, ibid., Through the Valley of the Shadow and Beyond

49. Rose Carson, full length, ibid. Camp Chesterfield, precipitated in 1894 for Dr. Carson of Kansas City. Rose was Dr. Carson's second wife

50. St. John, ibid. James Coates

51. Portrait of Audrey Alford with teardrop necklace and corsage dematerialised.

I now give a few concrete cases from their mediumship:

Mr. John W. Payne
Director, The Citizens Bank
New Castle, Indiana

It was made in the daytime in an ordinary room that was not darkened. The frame containing the canvas set on a stand before the window. Mrs. Charles Payne and Mr. John Weesner, who do not believe in Spiritualism, were with me, and we sat within five feet of the picture. The two Bangs Sisters, the mediums through whom the likeness was produced, sat at either side of the table and supported the frame, each with one hand. No brushes, paint, crayon or other substance of any kind was used as far as we could tell, and it was light enough to have seen a pin on the table. The sisters had never seen or heard of my father, nor a photograph or likeness of him. *All they asked was that I fix his features in my mind.* The picture was not made in spots or a little at a time. At first it was a faint shadow, then a wave appeared to sweep across the canvas, and the likeness became plainer. It was a good deal like a sunrise—got brighter until it was perfectly plain and every feature visible. Until the picture was completed, the eyes were closed, and then they opened all at once, like a person awakening. It did not take more than a half-hour, and is the best picture of my father we ever had. I do not pretend to say how it was done, simply that the picture was produced before our eyes without the mediums having ever seen a photograph or other copy.

The picture of the late Mr. John Payne is now hanging in the Citizens' Bank, and the owner of the portrait is a level-headed business man, and one of the most substantial in Spiceland, Indiana.

Letter to the Bangs Sisters
From 122 Lancaster Avenue
Syracuse, New York

Our Dear Friends (for such we must call you),

The painting arrived safely, and to say that we are both well pleased with it does not half express our sentiment.

Our little darling looked just as though he was ready to step down and out of the frame, he is so natural. We fully realize no earthly artist could possibly produce such wonderful work. One cannot see where the picture is started or finished, so perfect is the blending of the colors.

We notice the appearance of a certain little ring on the third finger of his left hand, the partial request of his mamma's. This marvelous work has been a great revelation to us; one year ago we could hardly have thought this manifestation possible, and we feel very grateful to you for your efforts in securing for us such a wonderfully satisfactory likeness.

May you have grand success in all your coming years of your life, that we trust the Over-Ruling Intelligence may prolong to a ripe old age, that others may have similar blessings that we are in possession of through your instrumentality.

Very sincerely your friends,
MR. AND MRS. MILFORD BADGERO

There was, again, no likeness of this spirit subject or even a Kodak photo that existed, thus crushing, once again, the conjurer's and critics loud theory that the Bangs Sisters simply copied the photo beforehand and then secreted it into the séance room.

James Coates:

Particulars of this artistically finished portrait reached me from good sources. It was on exhibition at Leach's Opera House, Wamego, Pollawatomie County, Kansas, during the whole month of April 1910, where it was fully recognized by many persons, intimate friends and many others who knew the late Mrs. Leach. The matter was also fully reported, 28th April, 1910, in the *Wamego Reporter*, in the town where Mr. and Mrs. Leach are so well known.

The facts of obtaining the pictures are these: Mr. Louis B. Leach, desirous of obtaining the portrait of his wife, arranged to have a sitting with the Bangs Sisters. They were holding séances in a room on the fourth floor of 1200 Pasco, in Kansas City. Mr. Leach called upon them at 3.40, on 30th March, 1910. His wife, Mrs. Ella Leamon-Leach, had passed into the spirit world little more than three years before, and her personal appearance was not known to the mediums. About seven minutes' time was employed in discussing as to the style of picture which would be most appreciated. The following took place.

The canvas, on a frame 36 x 48 inches, was selected and placed before the window - which was four stories from the ground - in such a way that the light fell on the back of the framed canvas. The colors began to develop in about four minutes, particularly rose red, quickly followed by darker colors and green. In thirty-five minutes the picture was practically developed in the presence of Mr. Louis B. Leach and the Bangs Sisters.

The former states:

No pigments or colors were furnished. No human hand, agency, mechanism, or contrivance rendered any assistance to the spirit forces executing the work. In this picture there are trees, vines and flowers, with a depth of scenery that is not often observed in portraiture. It is a striking likeness of my late wife. The dress she wears is to me a well-known study in Parisian art fashion. The hair and eyes are perfect; the expression is hers; and in this beautiful picture the colors of the trees, vines and flowers are distinctly true. I pronounce it a good likeness and a gem of art.

- LOUIS B. LEACH

James Coates:

Since obtaining the above, Mr. Leach, writing on 30th April, 1910, from Wamago State Bank, to the Bangs Sisters, says:

I have engaged a photographer to take a negative of Ella's picture, and will send you a cabinet, as soon as they are ready. I am very glad to let you have the use of the picture, or help you in any way I can. Your success will do us all good. I hope your experiences will lead to prosperous issues. I believe they will. My admiration of your work is only equalled by my love of the cause of truth.

James Coates:

> On my application to Mr. Leach for a photograph of this painting, in his letter (4th December, 1910), he regretted he had none available, having given the last away, and added: "You may take it from me that I am in favor of the Bangs Sisters and their work, and nothing has happened to make me change my mind in regard to their genuineness."

James Coates:

> This gentleman is a man of standing in Wamego, where he is president of the Wamego State Bank of Kansas, and he is also proprietor of Leach's Opera House. I have a long list of names, including Dr. C. H. Carson and various prominent citizens of Wamego and Kansas City, to whom Mr. Leach is well known. But I think the foregoing statement is adequate.

Dr. C. H .Carson was the husband of the spirit Rose Carson in the portrait.

Quote:

> I am aware that, since the foregoing exhibition of the Bangs Sisters, (demonstration in front of a large audience at Camp Chesterfield mentioned earlier – Ed.) certain imitations have been produced in public and called "spirit paintings." I also know that Mr.Wm. Marriott, of London, Eng., says that he can produce them. Since his book was written, Mr. Hereward Carrington, another expert, declares that he has a friend who can do so. Were it worthwhile, I might give it more attention to these claims.

> Have they produced pictures *under similar conditions* to those obtained by the Bangs Sisters? For this there is no evidence beyond the usual expert assertions.

> Have they produced identifiable portraits of persons whom they have never seen? No.

> Have any of their productions presented evidence of intelligences *outwith* their own? The answer is in the negative.
>
> - JAMES COATES

Portraits Painted by Invisible Artists – Continued

Mr. G. Subha Rau, editor of the *West Coast Spectator*, Calicut, India (who is not a Spiritualist), visited America some two years before Vice Admiral Usborne Moore, and gives a detailed experience in the number for March, 1909 of the *Hindu Spiritual Magazine*. I do not propose to give his account in full. When he obtained the precipitated portrait of his wife, he had the photograph of that lady in his pocket, which, however, the mediums did not see. In his statement, which I summarise, Mr. Rau says: "I had heard that the Bangs Sisters could produce through spirit agency a portrait of any deceased person. I had found it hard to believe such a claim, and when I arranged to have a sitting for a portrait of my deceased wife, I did so with no little incredulity. The Bangs Sisters claim that they can get a deceased person's portrait precipitated on canvas even when no photographic or other likeness exists. In my case there was a photograph, which I was carrying with me. I took every care to see that neither of the mediums nor any of their friends saw it. At this sitting both sisters took part."

"In the course of conversation, one or the other would describe what she professed to see. *They saw apparently a life-size image of the photograph I had with me, and described it correctly in the details.* For instance, they saw that I sat; that my wife stood behind, with her hand on my shoulder; that her face was round; that she wore a peculiar jewel on the nose; and her hair was parted; that a dog lay at my foot, and so on."

"Incidentally, I may mention that they described visions of one who, from the description, could be my mother; a third, my friend with whom I had been trying to communicate, and so on. But to proceed, they asked me to pick out any two canvas stretchers that lay against the wall, adding that I might bring my own stretchers if I liked. I took out two which were very clean and set them on the table against the glass window. I sat opposite, and the two sisters on either side. Gradually, I saw a cloudy appearance on the canvas; in a few moments it cleared into a bright face, the eyes formed themselves and opened rather suddenly, and I beheld what seemed a copy of my wife's face in the photograph. The figure on the canvas faded away once or twice, to reappear with clearer outline; and round the shoulder was formed a loose white robe. The whole seemed a remarkable enlargement of the face in the photograph. The photograph had been taken some three or four years before her death, and it was noteworthy that the merely accidental details that entered into it should now appear on the canvas. For instance, the nose ornament, already referred to, she had not usually worn. Some ornaments were clumsily reproduced. One that she had always worn, but which was not distinctly visible in the photograph, was omitted on the canvas. I pointed out these blemishes, and as the result, when I saw the portrait next day, all the ornaments had disappeared. I was satisfied that the portrait had been precipitated by some super-normal agency. As soon as the portrait was finished, I touched the corner of the canvas with my finger, and a greyish substance came off. The portrait is still in my possession, and it looks as fresh as ever. I had omitted to say it was all done in twenty-five minutes."

James Coates:

The above remarkable testimony by a skeptic and an eye-witness must be of great weight. The fact of reproduction does not take away from the value of the undoubted psychic action.

Mr. Rau is perfectly satisfied that the portrait was a case of precipitation; that the photograph in his pocket was the basis of the likeness, and not any mental picture which he had in his mind. He is also certain that the Bangs Sisters are genuine psychics, and the phenomenon obtained through them arose through occult causes; but he did not think either his wife, or the spirits from whom he desired to hear, had anything to do with the production of this portrait.

In this case—and also demonstrated throughout many of the precipitation sittings and recorded experiences in this book—one can easily see the outstanding level of clairvoyance demonstrated on the part of the amazing Bangs Sisters. Even in modern times, 2014, I will venture a theory that there is, most likely, no one who can demonstrate even remotely, this level of Mental Mediumship. In the case of Mr. Rau's sitting, it is interesting and highly evidential that the spirit artists removed one of the ornaments from the portrait and, when he pointed out the "blemishes" to the spirits, they then removed all the ornaments.

Mrs. Lucy E. Adams
356 East 60th Street
Chicago, Ill.

Mr. Coates,

I have had very little experience with spirit photography, but I have for my friend, Mr. Ghose, editor of the *Hindu Spiritual Magazine,* obtained a precipitated picture of his son through the mediumship of the Bangs Sisters. Mr. Shishir Kumar Ghose will be interested in your book on spirit photography, and so will I."

- MRS. LUCY E. ADAMS

James Coates:

There was a desire expressed that I should investigate personally the powers of these ladies. I wrote the esteemed editor of the Hindu Spiritual Magazine, for as he,is a man of standing in Hindu society and lately honored by the Indian Government, I would highly esteem his testimony. I received the following letter from his son, Mr. P .K. Ghose.

Hindu Spiritual Magazine Office
Calcutta, September 29, 1910

Dear sir,

Your favor dated the 30th July. My revered father, Babu Shishir Kumar Ghose, has been lying seriously ill for the last two or three weeks; hence he could not reply directly to your letter. I am, however, enclosing you, by his direction, a full description as to how the picture was precipitated. If possible, we shall try to send you a photograph of the picture.

Yours very truly

P. K. GHOSE, MANAGER

The photographs were duly received, 7th December, 1910

I should much prefer to give the report in its lucid completeness, but lack of space compels me to summarise it. I may state in passing that it was owing to the successful personal experience of Mr. G. Subha Rau that Mr. Ghose was induced to try to get a portrait of his departed son. Mr. Ghose could not proceed to Chicago, and had to depute the mission to a most trustworthy resident in that city, viz., Lucy E. Adams, an esteemed correspondent.

From the testimony of Babu Shishir Kumar Ghose, referred to in Mr. Piyush Ghose's letter, I take the following: "Having heard from a friend of his experiences with the Bangs Sisters in Chicago, I determined to get, if possible, the portrait of my beloved son, Poyesh Kanti. I could not go in person, so I wrote to a very dear friend (distinguished for her exceeding piety and sound judgement), who resided in Chicago. I asked her to visit the Bangs Sisters and get me a picture. Not believing in mediums, she objected, having no desire to help me to throw my money away. I insisted, however, and sent her a photograph of my son, so that she should have decided and available means by which to identify the picture; *but she was not on any account to permit the sisters to have a glimpse of the photo.* She finally consented. Taking her own canvas, and accompanied by an intimate friend, Mrs. P., who had no faith in Spiritualists, she called on the Bangs Sisters.

"There was only one of the sisters present, by whom they were taken into a small room where there was one small window, which was open to the street. Before it the canvas was hung, so that the light fell on its back, enabling my friend and her companion to see how the picture was drawn. That window formed the upper part of a door. The canvas could not be affected from without. There was no space under the door through which anything could be passed. But in either case, any attempt from above or underneath would have been detected at once.

"It must be borne in mind that it was the side of the canvas away from the window on which the picture was precipitated. The two ladies sat before, and the medium stood on one side, touching it. Immediately they saw a cloud over-spreading the canvas, and by degrees the picture was finally precipitated in the manner described by Mr. Subha Rau, in the *Hindu Spiritual Magazine*, March, 1909. These ladies had a watch before them, and when three raps announced the completion, they saw it was finished in exactly twenty minutes.

"Any human artist would, in my opinion, take at least twenty minutes to select the colors and blend the tints. In this delicate work of art, no sign of brush-work is visible, no crudities, as in portraits painted by competent artists. It was not done by the coarse hand of a material being, but by some means unknown to artists on Earth. Most assuredly it was not done, drawn, or painted by the only medium present or by the witnesses.

"The question arises, was the picture a painting of my son as the subject, or was it from his photograph? It may be alleged that the medium saw the photograph clairvoyantly, and that the spirit artist saw it through her. This is supported by the fact that the picture is very much like the photograph. There is one little circumstance which suggests that the spirit of my son was the subject of the picture, and that is, the complexion is correctly given. The medium could not have known that from the photograph. The Hindus of the higher classes in Bengal have a peculiar complexion, which has its distinctive characteristics. Again, the sisters allege that they can get pictures precipitated in a similar fashion without a photograph. I have no reason to doubt the evidence; therefore I conclude that the painting was that of the spirit present, and not from the photograph. The evidence is also conclusive that the picture was not done by mortal hand, but was finished by occult means; by invisible intelligence or spirit."

James Coates:

The above account may have suffered a little by my curtailment, but the central fact stands; i.e., that an identifiable portrait of a departed was obtained through the agency of intelligent artists in the Invisible, by the aid of a medium. This is supported by the testimony of Mrs. Adams and her lady friend. The first was doubtful of the legitimacy of the procedure and the genuineness of the mediums; and the second, if not both, was a non-believer in Spiritualism. There is also the identification by the hitherto unseen photograph; that of the honored Babu; the testimony of his son and a brother of the departed one. If this were not enough, there is the united testimony of the adult members of possibly the largest family in India, consisting of Babu Shishir Kumar Ghose's immediate descendants; his brothers and their wives, children, and grandchildren; his sisters, their husbands, children, and grandchildren; together with not a few other relatives, with the servants and dependents of this great household.

My only comment is that, the fact of the painting as the manner of its accomplishment being established beyond doubt, and, while it may be possible that the departed presented an image of his bodily form to the psychic artist or artists for production, the factor of the reproduction of the unseen photograph cannot be excluded. It would still remain the portrait of an invisible produced by no mortal hand. This is the central fact, and to my mind the most important.

The Testimony of
Dr. and Mrs. E. H. Thurston

I give their account in full, as I consider the evidence of value, and of interest as being recent:
Hagerstown, Indiana, U. S. A.:

5th April, 1910

Desiring a spirit portrait of our daughter, who passed into the spirit life at the age of thirty years, and having viewed some of the results obtained for others through this remarkable phase of the Bangs Sisters' mediumship, we decided to make a test of it ourselves.

Visiting Chesterfield Camp, Indiana, we called upon the Bangs Sisters in their cottage and arranged for our sitting, the hour set being the following afternoon. At the stated time we again called at their cottage. Entering the séance room, and finding only three canvases, I selected two of them, took them out in the sunlight, in company with one of the Miss Bangs, exposed them for fifteen minutes to the strong rays of the noonday sun, examined the surface thoroughly to fully assure myself that they were not chemically prepared, at the same time to secretly mark them for identification. Returning to the séance room, I placed the canvas on the small table before a well-lighted north window, and by examination of table and surroundings convinced myself that everything was void of any and all mechanical apparatus.

The Bangs Sisters, seated on each side of the table, merely supported the canvas in an upright position with one hand, myself and wife being seated directly in front of, and not more than two feet from them. After sitting a very short time, a dark shadow passed over the canvas, followed by the outline of the head and body; then, to our wonderful amazement, the perfect features of our daughter appeared, with the eyes closed; a few more seconds, and the eyes opened and before us was the beautiful spirit of our deceased daughter, perfectly lifelike in every feature, and which has been instantly recognized by all who knew her when in earth-life. When the picture was completed, the identification marks previously spoken of showed that the canvas had not been tampered with in any way.

While the portrait has much the appearance of pastel work, we have since removed particles of the material or substance of which the picture is made, and find it perfectly soluble in water, without imparting any color whatever to the water, which is not the case in pastel work.

Being somewhat familiar with photography and photographic processes, especially solar print work, we are fully convinced that the picture is not the product of any photographic process, and we desire to say right here there was positively no evidence whatever of any trick, or slight-of-hand performance; everything was perfectly straightforward and honest, as far as the physical eye could discern, and we went away from the cottage at beautiful Camp Chesterfield more convinced than ever before of the continuity of life after death, and the beautiful philosophy of Spiritualism.

The Bangs Sisters will ever have our highest regards, for we believe they are thoroughly genuine and honest.

- DR. AND MRS. H.E. THURSTON

Dr. and Mrs. H. E. Thurston did not state whether they had a photograph of their daughter taken in life, but I assume that to be possible, as the doctor was himself a photographer. It does not affect the facts stated whether they had or not.

James Coates:

I now give an interesting case in which no photograph had been taken. The account, which I submit, was given by Mr. George C. Holland, of Ottawa, Canada. In light, 15th May, 1909 (after describing the procedure at the cottage of the Bangs Sisters, at Lily Dale Camp, the test measures adopted, and the fact that Mrs. Holland and himself had no photograph of their son in their possession), he says:

"First, a cloud seemed to roll over the face of the canvas and disappear. It was followed by other clouds, each time some of the color remaining on the canvas, until a background was formed. Then appeared a faint outline of a human head, which disappeared and reappeared several times before remaining on the canvas. Rapidly the features seemed to grow, and finally the eyes, which for a time were indistinct and apparently closed, opened, and remained open on the canvas. In about twenty minutes the picture was completed. In a general way it resembled our son, but it was not even a fairly good portrait."

James Coates:

All the foregoing was carried out in a well-lighted room, and executed with the sunshine directly bearing on the canvas, which was selected by the investigators, and the mediums had no intimation of what sort of portrait was desired. The test adopted was a remarkable one, namely, two canvases were held face to face, and the portrait of the son appeared on one of them.

The one point I wish to note was the failure to produce a good likeness of the son of Mr. and Mrs. Holland. It will also be remembered that they had no photograph of their departed son with them. Possibly, too, they had not a clear mental picture of him, or, what is most likely, the mother had one conception of him and the father another; and the spirit artists produced a composite picture of the two.

An Exhibition of Spirit Paintings
James Coates, cont'd

I have omitted, from lack of space, Mr. J. M. White's graphic report
of the great exhibition of over one hundred psychic portraits, and
allegorical pictures of scenes in the Invisible, done by these mediums,
held last January in Kansas City. Two of these have been held in the
Galleries of Psychic Art, in the Temple of Health, corner of 12th and
Washington Streets, Kansas City, Missouri—the one above-mentioned
in January, and the other in December 1910. These were visited by
thousands of people on both occasions. To one interested in divine
revelations, a view of these pictures would be ample reward for coming
thousands of miles to attend the Convention.

 As to the nature and character of the Convention, I have nothing to
say in these pages except that it was a remarkable one, where highly
intellectual men and women gathered together to discuss matters
of health and well-being. Among the objects which were discussed
was the building of the Temple of Light. In this temple a new system
of education was to be carried out. What is of interest to us is that,
in addition to the hundred odd pictures, done by the Bangs Sisters,
adorning four art parlors in the Temple of Health, there is the psychic
painting of the proposed Temple of Light.

Dr. Carson says:

"The photograph is taken from the psychic painting executed in
the Temple of Health. The Temple of Light will be of the Grecian-
Roman-Ionian school of architecture, adhering to the beautiful lines
of the ancient temples that were erected in the Old World, and which
withstood the ravages of time for hundreds of years. The Temple of
Light will be built in the form of a cross, with four fronts, each 210
feet long, and the dome of magnificent proportions will surmount the
center. The building will be four stories in height, and marble will be
the principal material of construction. Immense columns of granite,
40 feet in height, and nearly 6 feet in thickness, will be placed at the
entrance of each of the four sides. Broad marble steps will lead to
great bronze doors, which in themselves are beautiful works of art,
reproductions of the doors of one of the ancient Grecian temples..."

Coates:

I refrain from giving a detailed description of the internal arrangements of the proposed building. The fact of the deepest interest to me is that the designs and colorings, etc., of this building were obtained psychically, with strict attention to architectural technique, from which any qualified architect could form his plans. The Temple of Health is a large structure, occupying a prominent position in the city of Kansas, where D. H. Carson and his assistants have been carrying on a vito-therapeutic system of medical treatment for the last thirty years. No greater or stronger testimony could be given to the unique gifts of the Bangs Sisters than the collection of paintings within its walls, where they can be seen, including the original painting of the Temple of Light.

This thing is not done in a corner, for the Society of Scientific Revelation, which is to build the great Temple of Light, consists of a quarter of a million members. No testimony within the range of psychical research will, in my opinion, be greater.

The following letter of experience is from Mrs. Gertrude Breslan Hunt, of Norwood Park, Illinois, a well-known student of economical and social questions, who has lectured all over the United States on child labor and other like evils. Both for the supreme interest of the letter, and the prominent position of the writer, I give her letter in full:

Gertrude Breslan Hunt:

I take great pleasure in telling the story of my investigations into the phenomena of Spiritualism, begun only three months ago, yet revealing so much! I was a skeptic until that time, regarding the few people I knew who believed in such things with pity, perhaps slightly mixed with contempt, for their abnormal credulity and imagination. I am therefore all the more anxious to make the expiation for my former prejudice and dogmatism. After years of study and thought, I had given up the belief in a continued life after death; but last October, a dear friend, a loyal comrade, a brilliant but martyred friend of humanity, passed out under circumstances so terribly sad as to make his life a supreme tragedy. I had looked death in the eye for months that same year, and never quailed for myself, but now death seemed a terrible monster. If a beautiful and noble life of service and love toward humanity could be ended in such fashion; broken heart, wrecked hopes, ignominy and neglect heaped upon him, when the natural and just reward should be love, honor, health, long life, and every good and perfect gift, I said to myself: "If this be all, life is not worth living; I could only die damning so terrible a life and dare not wait to see my beloved husband and precious mother face such awful exigencies." In this hour of anguish the thought came of the claims of Spiritualism, and now I decided to "investigate." I went to the best mediums, and there learned that I was wise. While the body of our friend and comrade was being cremated, I went to the Bangs Sisters and asked for a letter. I wrote four questions addressed to my friend, folded five blank sheets of paper around my note, sealed all in an envelope, and placed it between two slates, in broad daylight; put strong rubber bands about the slates, and never took my eyes off it where it lay before me on a bare oak table, and under my hand. After a time, Miss Bangs, who sat back in her chair, not touching the slate, said I might open the envelope. I saw the writing through the envelope before I tore it open, for it was sealed and the seal undisturbed. I kept up my investigations, and finally decided, with the consent and cooperation of friends, upon getting a spirit portrait of our comrade, especially for a memorial meeting we proposed to hold for him. To me, this transcends all other phenomena, for you have something you can retain, carry away with you, and show to friends, and relate the wonder of seeing it produced.

I informed myself of the devices claimed to be employed in certain newspaper "exposures." I learned that the only negative of the deceased was destroyed, and I held the only copy in this State. I examined floor, table, windows, and every part of the room, and selected a life size canvas from a lot of fifteen or twenty. It was placed in a window, and I sat facing the canvas. I did not remove my eyes from the canvas, and would stake everything I possess that no hand touched that canvas after I placed it in the bright light of the window, until the picture was finished. Three pair of eyes showed on the canvas in different poses and places. The background appeared first, as though successive layers of dust had been thrown on, then in a few minutes the whole face appeared, with the colors of life. I criticized the pose, and asked for a full-face view. The whole face faded out and was rapidly sketched again. I was requested to take the picture out and set it on the floor in such a light as it would be likely to have when finally placed. I did so, and remarked that the hair was too light; and there, where it sat, I saw the shadows creep into the waves of hair and it darkened. I asked that more color be put into the cheeks, and the canvas blushed to the tint it now bears. The sleeves of the robe were corrected, and in two hours the picture was complete; and a competent artist has stated that he could not finish such a picture in less than three days, working eight hours each.

The mediums did not know the name of the person, whether man or woman, had never seen or known Dr. Burson, *never saw the photograph, and no chance to copy it.* I am therefore forced to conclude that life continues after death and that we may receive messages, and that this portrait is a spirit portrait. I have had many other convincing evidences, some of them in other cities where no one could possibly have known anything of me. Nothing has brought me so much happiness, except the hope of the Co-operative Commonwealth and the resulting abolition of poverty and incentive to crime, when I believe we shall all "feel the soul with us climb," and reach heights scarce dreamed of now, and probably evolve, so that each may communicate with those in the spirit world without the aid of any other medium.

- Gertrude Breslan Hunt

Here was a séance moment I would call a definitive example of the genuineness of the Bangs Sisters mediumship that no critic can possibly deny on any conceivable level. Mrs. Hunt controlled the slate sitting, her hands only touching them throughout; and what can we say of the precipitation sitting? She herself placed the portrait in the window, no hand of the Bangs Sisters touching it, and then she herself lifted it down and, while it was on the floor, mentally requested changes, which manifested in front of her. What more can really be said?

Coates:

Here we find the spirit artists responding to the express wishes of the still embodied friend of the departed, and they comply with her wishes and also produce as a spirit portrait a picture which can be, and was, identified by a photograph taken in earth-life of the late Dr. Burson. It does not make the spirit (produced) portrait any the less valuable, but more so, that Mrs. Hunt possessed a clear mental vision of the departed, and its independent identification from the unseen but solitary print in that lady's possession, strengthens the evidence. At this stage the question arises: Are these spirit portraits the portraits of spirits in discarnate state, or are they the portraits of something which exists—although invisible—on the psycho-metaphysical plane?

The Experience of Judge Levi Mock, and Mr. Ripley
of Duffton, Indiana as reported in
The Light of Truth
September 16th, 1905
By Dr. J. H. Annis

The judge selected a canvas from a pile of fifty or more on which the picture was to be made. This was all the preparation necessary. One of the sisters sat on either side of an ordinary center table, supporting the mounted canvas by one hand, while the bright sunlight shone in through the open window. Mr. Ripley and Judge Mock sat directly in front of, and about four feet from, the canvas. In this position they watched the development of the picture. First the outline appeared, then disappeared. Then it came again, and continued to grow brighter, lifelike features filling in. The eyes were closed; but to their surprise, they suddenly opened, and gave an expression to the face that they felt that it ought to speak. Up to this time, neither the Bangs Sisters had ever *seen the photo which Mr .Ripley had concealed in his pocket. But, upon his bringing it out, a comparison showed an exact copy.* In earth life, the friend usually wore a Masonic pin, but from some cause he did not happen to have it on when he sat for the photo. Mr. Ripley desired it on the painting, and so made a mental, not a verbal, request for it, and immediately it appeared upon the lapel of the coat, just as he used to wear it. All this occupied about twenty minutes.

Coates:

This is one of dozens of other cases I might relate with the Bangs Sisters that are just as good in their respective cases.

In the foregoing, we see that the invisible artists responded to a mental request, as well as producing a portrait of the deceased, a likeness similar to that contained in an unseen photograph.

The Evidence of
Dr. J. M. Peebles[17]

Coates:

Dr. Peebles, the genial veteran author and lecturer, who possesses
a worldwide reputation, has on several occasions testified to the
genuineness of the phenomena witnessed in the presence of these
gifted psychics. He requires no introduction. I have curtailed the
report received, making reference only to the precipitated painting:

Dr. Peebles:

Journeying on our way to the Pacific Coast, we stayed overnight in
Chicago, calling on the Bangs Sisters, with whom we had previously
corresponded.

Though expressing their unpreparedness, they gave us a séance. We
were admitted to the séance-room, which had a large window at one
end, a door at the other, and two side doors.

Comfortably seated, conversation was genial and general, Dr. Peebles
desiring to have a spirit picture of one of his chief guides.

Mr. Sudall accompanied one of the sisters to a storeroom wherein
a pile of new canvases were stored. Selecting two of these from the
center, he marked them and carried them to the séance-room. We
examined the room, chairs, table, window, and shutters, finding them
to our satisfaction. Next, a curtain of black velvet was placed over the
window, and around the edges of the canvases, thus shutting off all
light, except that focused upon the almost transparent canvas.

With the sisters occupying seats on each side of the table, holding the canvas
near the window, and Dr. Peebles, Mr. Sudall, and a lady facing the front,
the conditions necessary for this kind of phenomenon were completed.

---

17   Dr. James Martin Peebles, (1822-1922), at age 22 was ordained a Universalist
Minister and preached in Kellogsville, Oswego, and Elmira, New York; was
a physician, prolific author, wrote *Seers of Past Ages*, 1820; *The Yearbook of
Spiritualism*, 1871; *What is Spiritualism*, 1903.

Soon the canvas assumed a gradually darker appearance around the edges. Now a change to light, and then dark again, wavering thus intermittently for a short time. Then came waves of seemingly colored clouds passing from side to side, up and down. Dimly we perceived the outline of a human head and shoulders; clearer and clearer they came to view, until the facial outlines were distinctly visible. Slowly, surely and gradually, with persevering effort, came the clear and distinct features of a patriarchal man with snowy white hair and beard. Suddenly the form vanished; and, clouding again, the canvas was almost a blank! Patient watching revealed to us the careful unfolding of the same remarkable features; the eyes were more brilliant and the features more distinct. *But we thought the beard was short and somewhat scant; the moustache a little uneven; and so, without further ado, the eyes gradually closed and the picture again clouded, to be again restored to our sight, in all the glory and magnificence it was possible to conceive of.*

Brilliant and piercing were the eyes, beautifully tinted were the features, and the beard no longer scraggy, but long, wide, flowing profusely in snowy whiteness, a glorious picture to behold.

Later, the words: "The Apostle John" were added in one corner of the picture. So here was the Apostle John's picture, as he trod the earth, ministering to the people, teaching and being taught, emphasizing the love to God and man. The whole proceeding seemed like a miracle, filling us with a feeling of awe and wonder. We are grateful beyond measure in the happy possession of such a valuable work of spirit science and art.

Believing in the integrity of the Bangs Sisters, we express our sincerest thanks for their untiring efforts in the work of Spiritualism, and for the comforting and inspiring messages received from our loved ones.

ROBERT PEEBLES SUDALL
JAMES M. PEEBLES, M. D.
28TH SEPTEMBER, 1910

Coates:

While it is wholly impossible from an identification point to say whether this spirit painting is a portrait of St. John, in earth life, I accept the statement over the signatures of the doctor and Mr. Sudall as to the facts and manner of obtaining this picture. Whether it was a portrait of the Apostle or, more probably, that of a thought-picture in the mind of Dr. Peebles, psychically discerned by the mediums, or the Intelligences controlling, I cannot say. I, however, call attention to the fact that the beard, which was at first thought to be somewhat scant, was changed to correspond with the sitters' ideas of what the portrait of St. John should be; and from this, corresponding to what I know of Dr. Peeble's opinions, writings, and public addresses, I am led to the conclusion that the painting came from the spirit artists (operating through the mediumship of those remarkable psychics) as a precipitation of the doctor's ideal. I might even go a step further and say it was a reproduction of a mental vision impressed on the subconsciousness of Dr. Peebles by an Invisible. The fact of the painting I admit, but I neither believe it to be the portrait of St. John, nor can I conceive the possibility of the beloved Apostle having a distinctly American physiognomy. The valuable evidence by the venerable lecturer is admirably sustained by the few cases selected for this book. If the evidences given in these pages are sufficiently strong to furnish a *prima facie* case that human beings departed can be photographed, or have their portraits painted, why not St. John? But that this has been done, there is absolutely no evidence.

May Bangs:

This painting is of spirit precipitation the same as all our art work, but taken from the mortal, that is, the subject still in earth life. It is a most excellent likeness, thus showing that, if our artist guides can so closely and beautifully portray a perfect likeness of those in earth-life, why not of spirit?

Coates:

I produce—owing to their importance—the portrait and extract from Miss May Bangs' letter (10th October). I cannot answer the question. It is, however, a matter of fact—and the above is not the only instance of the portraits of embodied persons being precipitated—that portraits of the living and so-called dead have been obtained in this manner through these mediums is beyond cavil.

The evidence to my mind is conclusive as to the genuineness of the phenomenon of precipitated paintings, but not that the same are the portraits of our departed—in a state discarnate—but rather of something representing them in the Akasa or thought atmosphere of those who knew them, when the same portrait is not an idealized production of a photograph or a picture in existence on earth. It may be I am wrong; I am open for further information.

Many of these precipitated pictures have been done in a remarkably short time. I have been present when the direct paintings have been done by the late Mr. David Duguid in two to three minutes. The Bangs Sisters have obtained complete portraits in eight minutes.

I have submitted a few portraits with actual reports and attestations, but I have on my desk at the moment of writing over sixty recent cases out of hundreds. Those of which I have deliberately selected cover a sufficient period of time—five years or thereby to date—to give the reader a fair idea of what these precipitated spirit paintings are.

The half tones which illustrate the artistic work done through the mediumship of these psychics do not do justice to the original paintings. They, however, show how lifelike the work is. A good deal of the effect, however, is lost in the half-tone process.

All correspondents assured me of this fact:

There is and must be a great deal of difference between portraits precipitated in the light and photographs taken by camera of the departed, yet, while this is true, there are points of similarity. In both, the likenesses are obtained of persons *as they were once on earth*. Their features are reproduced. Recognition would be impossible otherwise.

All spirit paintings, not portraits, which I have seen, represented scenes on earth. Many direct paintings and drawings obtained through the late Mr. Duguid were of this character.

Some drawings (not all), were line-for-line reproductions of drawings extant. The spirit-painted portraits of the Bangs Sisters are best obtained:

1st. When the person desiring the portrait is able to carry a clear mental picture of the departed; or

2nd Has a photograph of the departed on his or her person, although the said photograph has neither been seen nor handled by the mediums.

Now, let it be noted:

1st Whoever or whatever are the subjects of these portraits, whether they are of the departed, or mental pictures psychically obtained, or of actual photographs, etc., they must have been clairvoyantly perceived either by the Bangs Sisters or by the Intelligences in the Invisible using their medium-psychic faculties.

2nd However produced, these portraits were not painted by the hands of man, and by no process—not even solar prints —known to artists.

I therefore conclude we have reached the bedrock fact: That these precipitated paintings are the work of human intelligences operating on psychic planes, and through the agency of appropriate media. In the unique phenomenon of these remarkable spirit-produced paintings, the Bangs Sisters, in the history of the world's psychics, stand alone.

- JAMES COATES

The Testimony
of John S. King
Founder and President
The Canadian Society for Psychical Research
27, April, 1912

Quote:

....waves of color, mixing with the shadow...all in motion...like small wavelets, or ripples on an almost placid lake....and creeping, or rather *rolling upwards, one after another,* in orderly succession…as if striving slowly to attain the top.…

- JOHN S. KING

The Process of Spirit Painting

The day was fine and beautiful, that is the sun shone bright, the time between one and two p.m., the 27th April, 1912. The twin houses of the Bangs sisters had undergone artistic renovation; and paper, paint and varnish of human selection, had been employed by skilled renovators and decorators. The room, a Southern one, had but a single window, but it was bare of blinds and curtains, no pictures on the wall, no bric-a-brac about, no chair or seat or furniture at all; the room contained but odor, light and air, as we entered in; and as the sisters worked at replenishing, I watched, to learn just what was necessary, before we settled down. A light and empty table was first brought in, and placed near the only window, at the southern side of the room; and next were placed three common chairs, on three sides of the table, the east and west for them and the northern one for me. The pastel, cards, or canvases, or whatsoe'er their name, which were prepared, or stretched or mounted on wooden frame or rack, were next brought in, some six or eight; and placed at western side, and northern end of room. There were no spirits in sight, nor smiling "angel forms" and no other articles in view, save a dark colored curtain, and its purpose will be made known soon. So the work of preparation was now nearly through; and as there was no darkness, and therefore vision clear, I was permitted to make my own selection of the necessary two canvases, out of a group before alluded to; and such I brought as I selected them; and the bright light of day was shining in on them, and also through them, for they were not opaque. The position in which they were placed may be thus specialized.

I have in mind the one I want, I said, for such can read my thoughts; and if the work be done by spirit true, 'twill come just as I now desire; and so I looked upon these two sisters, and quiet sat, with watch in hand to note the time, which was half 'tween one and two; and gave my strict attention alternately to hands and arms of sisters both, and canvas before my face; and all within the area of the angle of my central fixed vision; while I felt a glow of subconscious knowledge elevating, which seemed to indicate, as if by intuition, that he, my friend Stead, [18] was now coming; and I gazed most critically upon the pure white canvas, with full light of day on front and back of it, and watching from my favored position each change, however slight, in motion or position of the psychic sisters; and I was as well extremely quiet, and motionless and listening, and could have almost heard the flappings of the wings of a butterfly in air, or the breathing of a humming bird, as I was constantly on the qui-vive of great expectancy; and so anxiously watched for the slightest indication of the work of spirit artist, no matter what moment, nor in what position it may appear.

Very presently just two feet from me, I noticed beginning change, from clear white on surface of the canvas, to that less clear, and on from that to faint shadow, slight evidence of waves of color, mixing with the shadow, and all in motion, like small wavelets, or ripples on an almost placid lake; and creeping, or rather rolling upwards, one after another, in orderly succession, as if striving slowly to attain the top; and then a portion in one place would deepen in shade, making form; and this with other delineations came into view, and slowly filling in with light, or darkness here or there, and colors more and more in evidence, along with apparent movement, and eyes forming, as if closed in sleep, or to emphasize the "Dawn of (his) Awakened Mind," and before me, as natural as he could be, I saw and recognized the face of William T. Stead, who wrote to me through the Human-Psychic-Telephone (Miss Maud Venice Gates), near Buffalo, at 4:30 p.m., 18th April, that he would try and show himself to me; and who at that same night at 10:00 p.m., came from the cabinet at Jonson's (Ben Jonson, materialization medium), in Toledo, western side of Ohio State; in transient body, clothed as he is in this spirit picture of him, and crossed the room to me, to prove as he has once more done, that he, my friend and co-worker, in human life, still lives and returns, and thus proves continuity. He surely fulfilled his promise to meet me in Chicago.

---

[18] William T. Stead, (1849-1912), editor, publicist and champion of Spiritualism; founder of the *Review of Reviews*; automatic writing medium, published *Borderland* in 1893; published *Letters from Julia* in 1897 under title, *After Death*; passed to spirit life on the Titanic, April 14, 1912, and communicated three days later in direct voice through the mediumship of Etta Wriedt.

On the following day another message came from the same source, hundreds of miles distant, and from it I also quote:

Well brother King be sure I'll bring you every proof I can (prediction). I am glad the artist of the Bangs sisters pictured me (prediction fulfilled), ..…and the whole of us together decided that my picture would be of use to your book,[19] as it would go to show that it is true that I, a discarnate spirit, known through the press to many men, may so come back in touch with life, and show my face to them. More dreadful than the wave that struck my life from me with final blow, is that great hatred of this truth, that we dear brother King are trying hard to make the living see.…but smiles of God's approving Son will be with us who suffer most; and we are both of us upheld by truth's great majesty. In all thy work, I am with thee.

Hypatia, (guide of Dr. King), whose form, voice, and personality have been observed by many hundreds of people in America, as well as by a well-known author in England, gave me her views regarding the spirit picture of Mr. Stead, by utilizing the Human-Psychic-Telephone, [20] and those views are recorded here.

Beloved one, I'll try to tell how it was done. Rembrandt in spirit paints the picture here, and it held aloft in *psychic ray*, and on the canvas is repeated, so the colors come to stay. *Hermes,* the levitation ruler, of the earthly powers to do, repeats exactly on the canvas, what *Rembrandt tells him to.* It is done by a repeating from light to heavy tone. The short waves become long waves.…Hermes like a town clock, keeps time exact in key with Rembrandt like a Swiss watch held, so it shows to him. Hermes like a set picture of fireworks, does so attune himself, that he can be repeater of the thing that he in Rembrandt's picture sees. It is like clay-moulder, copying a picture shown to him. 'Tis a process very beautiful, and much admired by me, and I encourage you to say twas

---

[19] *Dawn of the Awakened Mind*, John S. King, M.D., The James A. McCann Company, 1920

[20] Miss Maud Venice Gates, of New York State, defined to be "The Human Psychic Telephone," with automatic action, including movement, writing and speech; whose conscious and subconscious minds , act independent of each other, without clashing or confusion. A brilliant and unique automatic writing and speaking medium, and clairvoyant.

free from fraud in every way. Let critics talk, I look on with pride, and aid you through to prove to men that it was true.'

From Hermes: (A levitation spirit)

Hermes, I am, Bangs Sisters did not do it. The artist could not do it, though wise he be. I Hermes help the labor. I do it with a tone of heavier octave that is now Rembrandt's own. Light is a wave of substance, and I from nature's own great kingdom of the clay kinds, make pigments of my own. I do it, as Marconi tower I make myself to be, and what Rembrandt suggests as best, I answer real to him, or in the tone of painting that is preserved by thee.

John King:

At 2.15 p.m., June, 1912, a spirit intelligence who signed his name as Rev. Theodore Parker wrote: "I wish to give this word to you that I believe that it is true all you have said: and if I can, I'll aid to so enlighten man, that men abroad in every land shall look at it, and understand what had been as mist before, will come out clear and plain; and you will be successful in trying to explain. Bangs sisters are not fraudulent. I stood where I could see, and I approve of what you've done in every degree. For all eternity the men of enlightened thought will proudly speak of thee; and as I feel great love for you, receive this word from me.

A Criticism of William T. Stead's Spirit Picture
By J. B. Duncan: a Relative.
Toronto, 23rd February, 1912
To John S. King, M .D.
Elliott House, Toronto

Dear Sir,

I have now before me a large picture, purporting to be one of my cousin, the late W. T. Stead; and a photograph, said to be taken from same. I do not consider either the picture or photograph to be a faithful likeness of my late cousin, although *there is a very strong suggestion of his face, in both of them, particularly in the expression about the eyes, and in the firm set of the mouth. I may further say that the moment I saw the large picture, I knew at once it was, or at least was intended to be, one of my late cousin. It is five years since I last saw him; and I further understand, the picture referred to is alleged to be a spirit picture, and not one of a living human.*

Yours very sincerely,
E. J. B. Duncan

(Italics were Dr. Kings.) Note by Dr. King:

On the occasion of Mr. Duncan's view of the spirit painting of Stead, he exhibited a photograph of Stead procured some five years previously, which served him in his *critique*. When Stead came to me accompanied by Julia Ames, his guide, in the séance held by Mrs. Wells, he appeared with features more nearly resembling the photograph than the spirit painting; while elsewhere in the book he (Stead), especially calls my attention to the fact that he so appeared to illustrate that his features at that time were correct on the photograph, just as at the present time his features are equally true to the complete spirit painting. J. S. K.

Dr. King:

Regarding Mr. Stead's picture, each reader will form his or her own opinion, and will be entitled to know mine. Had he in mortal life selected the best two artists in Europe or America to paint his portrait and bust, I think it will be conceded that, even with the same pose for each of them, and working from the same point of view, they would neither of them be an exact duplicate of the man, nor yet a perfect duplicate the one of the other.

I think it will likewise be granted, that no artist whosoever could produce his second picture of him, doing it entirely from memory. So too it will be readily conceded that no two photographers can produce, under similar circumstances, a picture which will duplicate the other photograph in every detail. But the similarity of picture, and its original, constantly undergoes change, so that if we were, a year or two later, to make the comparison, this difference would be more apparent, even strikingly so with the constantly changing original, as the years pass away; so that it is in ordinary experience, often changed to so marked a degree, as to cause doubt to arise in the observer's mind as to whether two pictures represent the same original.

In the absence of two such pictures of the late Mr. Stead, while a mortal, I have illustrated this assertion by giving a photograph of myself at the age of 65 years, which will be found at the end of the chapter; and another one at the age of 70 years, at the beginning of the book. But supposing the spirit picture in all its natural coloring, from which this half tone engraving is made, to be a copy of another painting, or an original, then challenge its production, and prove my statement wrong. Until that day is done, I rely on Stead's statement that no such picture is in existence. The pictures everywhere, recognized as Stead's, were pictures of him in mortal life, at different times. Nor am I aware that spirit artists ever make pictures of men in earth life; or if so, I have no knowledge of it as a fact. Stead's picture had not prior existence; but it was produced in conformity with a promise made to me by himself as a spirit, and its production was complete in my presence a fortnight after he passed to spirit life, in a manner already described by me. He has confirmed this as fact through the trumpet and in the hearing of others.

CHAPTER 4

CONCLUSIONS & PERSPECTIVES

————————◦◦◦◦————————

"Nothing is too Wonderful to be True, if it be Consistent with The Laws of Nature."

~ Michael Faraday

Vice Admiral W. Usborne Moore
Circa., 1912

The world is not ripe for a general declaration of all the glimpses which diligent investigators enjoy of the world to come; it is unwise of any man to give out to a doubting crowd the sacred details which constitute his most cogent reasons for the faith that is in him. As long as nine-tenths of the inhabitants of the civilized world are in the unprepared, ignorant, and priest-ridden condition they are in now, such revelations would be productive of more harm than good, for they would, even in England, elicit anger, contempt, and ridicule. It is not the duty of an investigator to provoke such a result. His function is to state, as clearly as his idiosyncrasies allow, all that he has seen and heard, apart from family matters and intimate conversations with friends, and leave the consequences to those who read his account. It is not his business to concern himself with whether his readers believe him or not, nor to enter into any sort of propagandism.

Spiritism has been in the air for four thousand years at least, but not yet has the time arrived for it to be fully assimilated. It will come more quickly in Great Britain than America; but in neither country will it take deep root for many years—perhaps not before the end of this century. Backwards and forwards will flow the tide of belief and the ebb of angry denial until, after many long decades, a general agreement will be arrived at.

At the age of sixteen I entered the surveying branch of the Navy, and remained connected with the hydrographic department of the Admiralty, in some form or the other, for thirty-five years. When I left I had commanded six surveying vessels, and had been in charge of surveys in the Pacific Ocean, Australia, China, and on the coasts of Scotland and England. The life of a nautical surveyor is one long training in the powers of observation; there is no profession where so much is required of the eyes—very few where so much is demanded of the ears. The human eyes, looking straight in front of an observer, take in with more or less precision all objects within an arc of one hundred and sixty degrees. Those within eighty degrees can be seen with considerable accuracy. It is the business of the explorer to note what he can see at a glance within this arc; it is he who achieves skill in this line who succeeds in the art of chart-making and the collection of notes which go to make up the information required for the navigation of ships for long distances as well as short, good natural powers of observation, and of noting what he sees with accuracy, else he will fail in this particular profession. I did not fail.

My quest, since I retired, has been to ascertain whether or not there is a field of consciousness around us inhabited by intelligent beings who think as we think, talk as we talk, who have memories and terrene knowledge; who can identify themselves as people we have known, and consequently can be reasonably termed the discarnate spirits of those who were once dwellers upon this earth. This quest requires all the powers of observation, which an investigator can muster: it is a difficult study, often very baffling, full of disappointments and apparent inconsistencies. Careful records, critical analysis, and acumen are needed; much the same qualities as are demanded of the naval surveyor. The one occupation is not a bad introduction to the other.

My natural powers of seeing and hearing are now much the same as those of the average man of my age, but I am of the opinion that the occupation of my life afforded me the sort of training which is required for psychic investigation. I started with no desire for consolation and no preconceived views on the subject of occult study. In short, I believe my records are as much to be trusted as those of any of my predecessors who have devoted much time to this most fascinating branch of research.

I am aware that if had published this book sixty years ago, possibly even at a more recent date, it could have been successfully used against me as evidence that I was insane......

Did Anyone Catch the Bangs Sisters in Fraud?

It is a troublesome aspect within the records of Historic Spiritualism that in the case of the Bangs and, actually many other mediums of that age, there is such a limited amount of rare source material to utilize. I am lucky that I found what I did. In light of this, after having spent a number of years gathering material for these Chicago mediums, I can at least comment on what I have unearthed and I must say that it is a curious fact that we have only Rev. Krebs and Hereward Carrington's reports of fraud that stand out, as such, and both involved their sittings for independent writing. Carrington, by the way, published his fraud theories without allowing Dr. I. K.Funk, who hired him to investigate the Bangs, and Admiral Moore, to read the report first. (The Society of Psychical Research, relying on unfounded statements, also spread the report of fraud.) We must ask ourselves why would Carrington not have informed at least Mr. Funk immediately of his findings? On the other hand, I have no definitive, credible reports of any act of fraud committed during a sitting for precipitated spirit portraits. There are theories, yes, as we shall see, but nothing conclusively proving fraud. A theory falls in the face of a fact. Under the *same exact conditions* that were employed by the Bangs, no one who has ever challenged their phenomena has ever achieved the same results. If so, where are the reports of this? I am not referring to the Campbell Brothers who did not challenge the legitimacy of the Bangs nor to the burlesque versions of the conjurers.

For Carrington to actually believe that Abbott had duplicated the Bangs, insinuating that they were using the same conjuring method over and over again for all of their portraits mainly by substitution, is audacious, outlandish and simply impossible to believe. Mr. Abbott's theories were born exclusively from his imagination based on the simple fact that he had never actually sat with the mediums. I did not see any elaborate explanation included in his work on why he challenged the mediums but never took the time to meet them. Why not go to Chicago and book a sitting with them? Is that too much to ask or did he know what the results would be if he did? On the other hand, Rev. Krebs hyperbolic imaginations would be better suited as a single chapter in a Magicians Handbook entitled: "My Imaginary Slate Writing Séance with the Bangs Sisters" or, "An Idiot's Guide to a Fake Séance." Reverend or not, I have *never* believed a word of it. Did Rev. Krebs stand up and immediately stop the sitting and charge over to the "door" where he indicated May Bangs may have been hiding, and simply catch her in the act? Apparently not. Are we to also believe that Lizzie Bangs could be so stupid to not have seen Krebs staring down from his chair with his tiny hidden mirror, watching her from under the table while the reflection—so-called—would be upside down? Is this what Krebs actually expected people to believe? There is also the issue of how May Bangs, if hidden behind the door, could actually have answered his letter. The blank pages of all their independent writing were usually covered with writing by the spirits. Are we to also assume that all of the answers were 'made up' on the spot by May Bangs? Did Krebs ever publish what the slate writings actually said? It is another mystery that seems to elude us.

It was these preposterous assumptions made by these individuals that, not only the Bangs, but all of the other credible witnesses could be such imbeciles that ruin their charges forever. Did Mr. Carrington ever receive an actual portrait when he visited them? No. Most likely his hostile attitude towards the experience brought its own results. Did Carrington ever demonstrate his ability to do "slate writing" in front of the Bangs, Admiral Moore, or Dr. Isaac Funk under the same, exact conditions as he stated he could? No. Did Abbott ever demonstrate his conjuring method of the spirit portraits in front of the Bangs Sisters with witnesses? No. But did he, after not having had the literal experience of seeing the phenomena of spirit precipitated portraits, publish the "Final Solution" to the spirit portrait mystery? Yes, I am afraid so. And lastly, considering the Bangs independent slate writing, did any of these critics ever intelligently explain how, unless by pure clairvoyance, the Bangs could know, *within moments after sitting down*, the contents of the sealed letters?

For me, as one outstanding example, I certainly believe in the conclusions of Admiral Moore. If he had used these same powers of skill and acute observation to uncover fraud on the part of the Bangs Sisters, I would have believed in those conclusions all the same. I also believe in the eye-witness reports by people such as May Wright Sewell, Gertrude Breslan Hunt, John W. Payne, the signed witnesses under oath of the Indiana Association of Spiritualists, Mr. and Mrs. Badgero, Louis B. Leach, Mr. and Mrs. Audrey Alford, the testimony of Babu Shishir Kumar Ghose, the Thurstons, Dr. C. H. Carson, Dr. J. M. Peebles, the report of Mrs. Lee Baxter, Dr. Carpenter, S. J. Gibson, Lyman C. Howe, Dr. Isaac K. Funk, George Drummet, and the unnamed thousands who were out there and experienced the same thing; you can rest assured they were there. I only wish that many others would have had their experiences published.

In the case of David P. Abbott, I give him credit for the seemingly inordinate amount of time and energy he spent in trying to convince the public —after having recanted his first official theory that he published—that the Bangs Sisters' precipitated portraits were nothing more than an elaborate, "David Copperfield" type, stunning trick, played on the thousands of people that came to them for sittings. He falters though in his official presumption that all of the portraits were done using the same, intricate methodology, i.e., portraits prepared beforehand by copying a photograph that the sitters had left with the Bangs a few days before, etc. This theory is crushed by the numerous eye-witness reports from reputable people who were on the alert and, contrary to Abbott's thinking, intelligent enough to discern the experience and see for themselves that it was highly legitimate and verified through their own senses. There are reports of the portraits changing afterwards, and reports of the Bangs never touching the canvases in numerous instances, an outstanding example of which is the live demonstration at Camp Chesterfield in 1909. The Bangs had no photograph of the spirit who precipitated, and, are we to assume that Mr. and Mrs. Alford, who were not Spiritualist in belief, would have actually handed over a photograph to people they did not even know, let alone trust, before the event? A select committee picked the canvases beforehand, and the Alford's saw and experienced their own daughter, Audrey, manifest on to the canvas. That is, without any doubt, what took place. The before and after photos of Audrey speak for themselves. The reports filed by James Coates as another example: are we to doubt the words of these witnesses?

Next we have the issue of how the Bangs Sisters could actually "paint" a portrait beforehand. Did any of these critics and experts actually catch the Bangs Sisters doing this? Did they burst into the Bangs' house and find all the paints, artists materials, and airbrush machine? Did they see and report any residual substance on the floor of their house for instance, dust or pastel matter on the furniture, or anywhere? One would think that, if this elaborate scheme was carried out, there would certainly be indications of it *somewhere*, even to the minutest degree. Some simple forensic detective work could have solved that mystery by employing a basic magnifying glass. But what about the actual so-called "magic demonstration" of the portraits being carried out? Did anyone ever just stop the séance and expose the sisters in the act of moving the blank canvases backwards and forwards while the finished portrait was in between? Why have we no proof of this? Because none exists. The outrageousness of the theories against the Bangs' legitimacy almost equals the wondrousness of the phenomenon itself.

There are serious questions laced in between all of these fraud theories, around every turn of the road. In the section involving excerpts from Mr. Abbott's book, he mentions the English conjurer, Mr. Selbit, who was under the authority of a Mr. Wilmar, of London; also there is mention of "the great American magician," Mr. Howard Thurston, Henry Clive, another English conjurer, and W. J. Nixon, known as the "Master Mind of Modern Magic," and the list of these renowned individuals goes on. Mr. Selbit, mentioned above, advertised his performance saying that it was spirit artists reproducing famous paintings, etc. These stage conjurers did not give a hoot if the Bangs Sisters were genuine or not; what the Bangs Sisters' phenomenon did was supply all of them with a new, awe inspiring idea, and new material for their live demonstrations in front of large, enthusiastic audiences. The Bangs Sisters were nothing to them. Catching them at fraud was not the issue. Creating what was nothing more than a burlesque version of their phenomenon was their imagined accomplishment. On another interesting note, the conjurers and amateur magicians throughout Spiritualism would never criticize each other but would, by unleashing their mob mentality, unceasingly criticize the mediums. It was also a bit amusing that the methods that were, according to David Abbott, invented by him to show how the portraits were done, were immediately absconded by certain of his fellow magicians and used on stage. He was ripped off right under his nose it seemed.

Who Sat With The Bangs Sisters?

Within the whirlwind of all of the magicians and their elaborate stage productions, fame and notoriety, let alone the vast sums of money being made, all one needs to ask oneself within all of this grandstanding is if any of these greatest of performers had ever actually witnessed a spirit precipitation with the Bangs Sisters? I can hear the same answer echoing again from the halls of truth. ... No. None that was documented that I ever saw or read about.

Also, and most importantly, if the Bangs Sisters were not mediums, why put themselves through the unending trauma, public abuse, hostility, ridicule and scandal, day after day after day, unless they were genuine? Why would they subject themselves to being accused of being two of the greatest impostors in history? Why not just be "The Great Bangs Sisters, Masters of Illusion" and make millions from their stage show? The conjurers had universally acknowledged their precipitated portraits to be 'the most miraculous phenomenon that ever confronted them'. Why admit to something you are not? If I may digress briefly, the Davenport Brothers, Ira and William, when touring through the towns of Phoenix, Mexico, and New York, in 1859, were confronted by the medium-hating township officials that demanded the Davenports apply for a Magicians License, so-called-first, before any demonstrations. They refused, saying that they were not magicians and would do no such thing. When threatened with jail, they chose jail and, of all things, were locked up in my hometown's county jail, in Oswego, New York for an astounding 29 days. Instead of renouncing their mediumship, they chose the way of truth, similar to the Bangs Sisters.

In the case of Hereward Carrington, he gave a false name for himself and to the individual he wanted to hear from during the independent writing sitting he attended: an immediate condescending, vibrational insult to the proceedings. Granted, he asked for a letter from his dearest mother, "Jane Thompson," and received a reply from that individual, to "Harold," his fake name in turn. This proves that he did actually receive a reply from the person he wanted, whoever it was. He lied, therefore, and, within the proven séance law of reversed conditions, the spirits may very well have lied back. Did he, Carrington, get up from his chair if he suspected something and catch the medium and her sister confederate who, he may have assumed, was hidden behind the infamous "Rev. Krebs door" during the sitting—since he presumed that Krebs theory was correct—and actually catch the mediums in the deception? The answer again, is no.

On another note, I myself, within the last twelve years have sat with four of the best known British physical mediums. All of them were genuine, to a certain degree, as I will explain: Two of these my wife and I invited to our home in New York to test their mediumship; one for two weeks and one for three months. Under our own conditions, with the mediums having been cable-tied to their chairs with no possible means of getting free[21] we have seen spirits materialize, and have had conversations with spirits through the trumpet which was hovering in the air at times eight to ten feet from the cabinet where the mediums were sitting.

In light of Mr. Carrington's report, I have this to say: I have been addressed by individual spirits who, in one instance, claimed to be the famous Seneca Wolf Clan Chief, Red Jacket, and most mysteriously on another occasion by an individual who indicated in a most solemn manner, that he was Sir Winston Churchill. Did I actually believe that it was the individuals who they said they were? Absolutely not for an instant, there being no proof of it whatsoever. But did I believe the phenomenon—spirits manifesting and speaking—was actually happening? Without any question, yes.

Mr. Carrington's report validates the *manifestation having happened* with the Bangs Sisters, and also validates the fact *that liar and impostor spirits can slip in*, and do. Why could he not have simply *told the truth* and written a question for a spirit he knew? The results, no matter what the outcome, would still have been worth reporting I am sure. His report does not prove fraud; it proves that he himself assumed it, and assumptions are not proof. Again, the case is weak; thus it has to be eliminated, in my opinion, as positive, verifiable proof of skullduggery against the Bangs Sisters. It is easy to see that all of the most famous insinuations against these mediums were based on conjecture, not on facts.

---

[21] We had also experimented with no cable ties used whatsoever, with the same results.

I think it has been clearly, and logically illustrated, that the Bangs Sisters were, in this writer and researcher's opinion, genuine and true physical mediums of the highest level. There is simply no solid, substantial proof that successfully demonstrates the Bangs Sisters' being otherwise. The fraud theories, all of them, are littered with *Reasonable Doubt.* In light of this Titanic Truth, the Bangs Sisters would never have been found guilty in any court of law and that fact speaks wonders if approached from any perspective. The phenomenon of precipitated portraits and independent writing was never duplicated under the same conditions to substantiate *any of these claims*, ever. Their mediumship should be respected for the glorious reality that it was and for the happiness that it brought to thousands of people.

Long live their name within the hierarchy of Historic Spiritualism, The Bangs Sisters, May and Elizabeth.

APPENDICES

APPENDIX A

T*he Spirit Zone of The Northeast*, originally published in 1994. Noah's Ark Society/N. Riley Heagerty

Over the years that I have collected rare books and done my research, it has been revealed to me, over and over again, that I was living somewhere near the middle of an area of the Northeastern United States, the Great Lakes regions to be exact (I live on Lake Ontario) that has produced an astonishing amount of physical mediums, many of whom were regarded as the most powerful and famous in America. I have included a simple map (List of Illustrations) in which I have outlined the Great Lake regions where many of the mediums were living and practicing, the heyday of which, as always, being the late 1880's and early 1900's.

The little dot near the middle of Lake Ontario, the upper of the two smaller lakes, indicates where I live. Less than an hour from my front door, is the site of the original Fox Cottage, Hydesville (now Hydesville Road), where Modern Spiritualism began in 1848, and, it is unknown by most that two hours west of the Fox site, in 1885, hundreds of people were gathered on the front lawn of the Davenport's home, in Buffalo, New York, to try to witness the extraordinary manifestations happening with the Davenport children, Ira, William, and sister Elizabeth within their home.

Spoken of by certain spirits, and taken note of by prominent researchers such as Vice Admiral Usborne Moore, is the fact that, combined with the cool, crisp and dry conditions of this Northeastern region of the United States, the Great Lakes themselves give off a tremendous amount of magnetic and electrical energy, greatly facilitating the production of physical phenomena.

Concerning physical mediumship and the phenomena associated with it, there are mysteries that we will never truly understand, but great bodies of water do seem to enhance physical mediumship. It is generally understood that some of the greatest artists, poets and musicians who ever lived were never discovered and made into "public" figures in their lifetimes. When this logic is applied to physical mediums, reclusive by nature, I personally believe that, concerning the Great Lake regions, just the tip of the iceberg has been revealed, as far as powerful mediums are concerned, and that the hundreds and hundreds more that were out there chose the safety and sanctity of their own home circles to remain forever out of the grasp of publicity and fame.

I am not surprised that right near the vicinity of the Davenport's home, was the mother of all waterfalls, Niagara Falls, pounding away. We also have all three of the famous Spiritualist towns, Lily Dale, sixty miles south of Buffalo, Camp Chesterfield, and Camp Silver Belle all within the magnetic energy of the lakes. The famous trumpet medium, Mrs. Etta Wriedt, was born in my hometown of Oswego, New York, and the Davenport Brothers gave demonstrations there at Mead's Hall. Here is a small and incomplete list, which I have compiled, over time, of the physical mediums who practiced and lived in "The Zone."

Mina Crandon: Physical phenomena, Boston, Mass.

The Fox Sisters: Leah, Margaret, and Katie, Rochester, rapping, materialization, Rochester, N.Y.

Ethel Post Parish: Materialization and trumpet, Camp Silver Belle, Euphrata, Pennsylvania

Elizabeth Compton: Havana, N.Y., materialization of forms, and complete dematerialization of medium; now Watkins Glen, N.Y.

Ben Jonson and Mrs. Jonson: Materialization, Toledo, Ohio

Ada Besinnet: Physical phenomena, Toledo, Ohio

Jonathan Koons and Family: Athens County, Ohio, the first recorded use of the trumpet in the first "Spirit Room."

James "Farmer" Riley: Materialization, Marcellus, Michigan

The Misses Berry, Helen, and Gertrude: Materialization, from Boston, Mass.

Frank Decker: Trumpet, Lily Dale

M. A. Williams: Materialization, New York City

William Cartheuser: Trumpet, New York/Lily Dale

James Laughton: Trumpet, Michigan and Indiana-Camp Chesterfield

Rev. Charles Swann: Trumpet, Indiana

Clifford Bias: Trumpet, Anderson, Indiana

H. B. Fay: Materialization, Boston, Massachusetts

Mrs. Emily S. French: Independent voice, Rochester, N.Y.

Dr. Henry Slade: Slate writing, Philadelphia, PA.

Mr. and Mrs. Nelson Holmes: Materialization, Philadelphia, PA.

The Bangs Sisters, May and Elizabeth: Spirit precipitated portraits, and independent writing, Chicago, Illinois

Robert Chaney: Trumpet, Independent voice, Indiana

Mable Riffle: Trumpet, physical phenomena, Indiana

Dr. E. A. Macbeth: Independent voice, independent writing, Rhinebeck on Hudson, N.Y., Camp Silver Belle, Euphrata, PA.

Dr. Robert Moore: Materialization, New York City

Anna Throndsen: Materialization, Indiana

Virginia Roberts: Physical phenomena, New York City

Maud Lord: Physical phenomena, New York City

Mary Murphy Lydy: Materialization, direct voice, Indiana

Mary Langley Beattie: Direct voice, materialization, Indiana

Mrs. Anne Keiser: Solar plexus voices, Buffalo, N.Y.

Maggie Vestal: Trumpet, Anderson, Indiana

The Eddy Brothers William and Horatio & Family: Materialization, physical phenomena, Vermont

The Davenport Brothers and sister Elizabeth: Physical phenomena, Buffalo, N.Y.

Mrs. Etta Wriedt: Trumpet/direct voice, Detroit, Michigan

And all of the other mediums from Lily Dale, Camp Chesterfield & Camp Silver Belle, Wonewoc and the hundreds and hundreds who I have not mentioned, or who kept it a secret, *I know you were there.*

APPENDIX B

———————⟫•⟪———————

Brief Synopsis of the book, *Marguerite Hunter*, written by independent slate writing with Lizzie Bangs & Illustrations in oil precipitated between slates by "Azur," guide of medium, Allen Campbell, of The Campbell Brothers. 1894. By N. R. Heagerty

The story of Marguerite Hunter is a sad one, but ended with her having produced her book *From the World of Spirit* with the aid of many in both the earth plane and the celestial realms.

She lived in the state of Kentucky, at Sulpher Well Village, in Jessamine County and was a young school student in 1844 right before the advent of Modern Spiritualism in 1848. During this time, she met and fell in love with a Mr. C. H. Horine, who was a teacher but, after a time, circumstances changed the course of events as he said: "Disproportionate circumstances soon led me to take a tangent course, and in 1846 I resigned my post as teacher. Pupil and teacher then parted as though they had never met, parted as lovers, but never then dreaming of the reunion which the future veiled from but nevertheless had in store for them..."

Twelve years had passed and, when he returned from his journey, he had found out that Marguerite had been married, but the union was a sad and terrible one due to the intolerant and savage temperament of the husband whom she had left several times and wanted a divorce from—specifically for the safety of their two lovely children. In a final fit of rage, the husband had confronted Marguerite in a field one day and, with the children watching, shot and killed Marguerite and then, in an equally terrible circumstance for the young ones to witness, shot himself.

Mr. Horine in 1890 moved to the city of Chicago and eventually—being a seeker after truth—became converted to Spiritualism. Four of his children were already in the Spirit World, so his senses and emotions were at that "certain pitch of Spiritual vibration." In that year, his children manifested to him through various media and, after awhile, in the month of December to be exact, Marguerite manifested and they relived their entire past through lengthy conversations. In December of 1892, in a lengthy independent slate writing session with Lizzie Bangs, she expressed the desire, when conditions were favorable, to form a book of her life in the material and spiritual spheres, and so, in 1892, the book was completed.

There's a few items that I want to clarify concerning this story that the readers, I am sure, will find quite interesting. It is a little complicated to explain, but I will do my best.

The author of the introduction who called himself "White Rose" stated that his guide in the spirit world dictated, "materially and inspirationally," the form of the book for the author in spirit life, together with the guides of Lizzie Bangs, who assisted the spirit band who transcribed the book in material writing and who called themselves, "Everlasting Unity."

"White Rose," was obviously a medium on the physical plane. M.C.H. Horine sat for the precipitations on porcelain with Allen Campbell and then stated that he sat with Lizzie Bangs three times a week at her home in Chicago. They began sittings in November, 1893 and ended on April 28th, 1894. "White Rose" stated that he had the pleasure of attending at least forty of these sittings. At each slate writing séance with Lizzie, six to eight pages of slate writing—similar to the ones photographed—were produced as Mr.Horine and Lizzie held the slates. Both Mr. Horine and "White Rose" testified to the total and absolute genuineness of the phenomena, control and conditions of the sittings with both Lizzie Bangs and Allen Campbell.

White Rose:

> The book, spiritual in its origin and lofty in its teachings, pervaded by a sweet and overpowering spirit of love, bearing its lessons of spirituality home to all, will be as a voice crying in the wilderness, but the writer writes, under the influence and inspiration of his beloved guide, this prophecy to the reader, "Blessed are the eyes that shall see and the ears that shall hear what is enfolded in the thought of these pages."

And she adds: "Dear reader, approach the open pages as you would the delicate bloom of a flower, not to mar or destroy, but the more reverently to appreciate a heavenly work. Accept its teachings and, by the more sensitively imbibing fragrance of its inspiration and its love, thus come more closely into oneness with the Divine."

- White Rose

APPENDIX C

———————————

R on Nagy: Researcher, author, Lily Dale Historian, and Museum Curator

People interested in the historic Spiritualist town of Lily Dale, should avail themselves the opportunity to go there and, while visiting, see Mr. Ron Nagy, who is usually at the museum, [22] fielding questions, of which there can be many, especially during the "season" which usually goes from July to September. Following in the footsteps of Mrs. Joyce Lajudice, who was the historian for many years and a friend of mine, Ron has an almost encyclopedic knowledge of Lily Dale's long, illustrious history, and matters involving mediumship and its various phenomena. He has published three books to date, between 2009 & 2011: *Slate Writing, Precipitated Spirit Paintings, and The Spirits of Lily Dale.*

He has been a good friend and comrade in the realms of deep research of Spiritualism. To know Spiritualism's history, one must know the 'players' involved in its long history, and it takes time to get there, lots of time. After Joyce's untimely passing, Ron took over the job of historian and we have connected since then, comparing notes and sharing historical facts. This form of research involves an almost incomprehensible level of patience and, at times, seemingly endless trails it takes to navigate in finding the answers, and Ron is one who understands this.

His work on Slate Writing, I consider the definitive work on that subject, and, as far as Lily Dale's amazing history, I can only wait and

---

[22] Ron Nagy can also be found at various times at the coffee shop, absconding with the last piece of their delicious carrot cake.

hope that a second volume is coming—in that regard—because his first published offering on the camp, mentioned above, is an absolute gem and should be required reading for all who want to know and understand Lily Dale.

His work on spirit precipitated paintings is a vitally important and comprehensive work involving the actual "science & chemistry" of how precipitated portraits are done, including—and very importantly so—a necessary, highly informative section on the incredible Campbell Brothers, the only other mediums that did precipitated spirit portraits. For the first time, in Ron's book, the medical reality of Iridology, the study of the Iris of the human eye and how it might pertain to precipitated spirit portraits is examined; it is indeed the beginnings of something that may change the course of psychical research as we know it. The work I have now done, specifically on the *Bangs Sisters*, would never have been complete without his aid and his true and legitimate love of this wondrous and eternal subject. Expect many more things to come from Ron Nagy; he is the real deal and, believe me, such people are hard to find.

APPENDIX D

—————⟫●⟪—————

The Education Of The Bangs Sisters: A Worthwhile Theory.
Material Supplied by Mandi Shepp, Director, Marion Skidmore Library, Lily Dale
Lily Dale Assembly

It seems unlikely that they would have enrolled in formal college of any kind; they weren't exactly from old money, they just seemed to earn their own way for most of their lives, and generally families who encourage their children to work at a very young age don't really see the need to send their kids away to school, especially during post-Civil War times. After doing some research, it doesn't seem as if Chicago really kept very good track of their school enrollment until the 1880's, when the population boom had kind of settled down and they could re-work their administrations; before then, a lot of new families and households were springing up, and it seems like keeping track of the population's minutia wasn't really their top priority; primarily birth and death records (death records are also spotty for these days, such as with marriage records: Mary (May) Bangs doesn't even have a formal death certificate.

It does, however, seem that during that time, there was only one major art institution in Chicago, the *Chicago Fine Arts Institute*. To assume that the Bangs girls enrolled there and learned this level of mastership in painting is a little too hard to comprehend at that age, let alone how it was paid for. Their father, Edward Bangs was a tinsmith, with four children to support, May, Elizabeth, Edward and William. It seems unlikely that he could afford much, let alone the enormous expense of a private fine arts school for two girls. They attended regular, elementary school and for how long, it is not known.

APPENDIX E

———◆———

T his next section is the controversial Addendum that W. Usborne Moore published in *Light* concerning the mystery of whether Hereward Carrington ever visited the Bangs Sisters house and received his famous reply letter from "Jane Thompson."

CORRECTION TO PAGE 625 "GLIMPSES OF THE NEXT STATE"
MR. HEREWARD CARRINGTON AND THE BANGS SISTERS
(From *Light*, December 14, 1912)

Sir,

As you have closed the correspondence on the above subject, I am not going to enter into any controversial matter, but merely to make a statement as an act of justice to Mr. Carrington.

In Appendix (C) to my book I have thrown out doubts of Mr. Carrington having been inside the Bangs Sisters houses. After discussing the pros and cons I wound up with the following sentence: "However, I would fain believe that, owing to so long a time having elapsed....the Bangs Sisters, may possibly have forgotten what sitters they received on a certain date.....let us try and credit that he *did* go to the séance room..." (P.625).

I am pleased to say that this pious wish has been translated into fact. A mutual friend remonstrated with me for doubting Mr. Carrington's *bona fides* and I suggested to him that there was a simple way of proving that his friend had sat with May Bangs. If Mr. Carrington would procure from Dr. Funk's executors the original letter that he found between the closed slates, I would compare the handwriting with that of my letters obtained in a somewhat similar way. This letter has been sent, and I have compared it: The writing in my opinion, is practically the same as in my letter.

I am, therefore, prepared to assert that Mr. Carrington did sit with May Bangs, and, in reply to a letter from himself to his "Dearest Mother, Jane Thompson" (who never existed), did receive a reply addressed to "Dearly Loved Son Harold" in affectionate terms, from his Beloved Mother, Jane Thompson.

As I took a number of precautions that Mr. Carrington did not, which included sitting between May Bangs and the suspected door, and using my own chemical ink, slates, marked paper, and so forth, I am as certain that my letters are genuine spirit manifestations as I am his was intended to make a fool of him.

Unless Mr. Carrington desires to pursue the controversy in some other journal, I do not propose to refer to the matter again. Dr. Funk is dead. *The Annals of Psychical Science* (English Version), is also defunct, and few investigators care a button about the matter. In the next edition of *Glimpses of the Next State*, I shall delete those passages which contained doubts as to Mr. Carrington having been in the house.

- W. Usborne Moore

APPENDIX F

———⟫●⟪———

Hereward Carrington's "Jane Thompson" letter, published in his book, *Personal Experiences in Spiritualism*, 1918.

My Dearest Mother,

If you are here, I trust you will communicate with me, and tell me anything you can of your life in any foreign country in which you lived. I hope the "Spirit Guide" of Mrs. Bangs may help to bring you, and assist you to write.

Your Loving Son,
Harold Thompson

Response:

Dearly Beloved Son Harold,

I am very happy to come to you in this way today, that I am with you always (sic), when your thoughts turn to me, and many times when you are engaged in the duties of life, alone and resting, the new-born spirit is free to come and go at will, distance or material objects from (form) no barrier, and as a mother's love and interest is intensified in the higher life, so am I drawn back to you constantly, while yet improving all the opportunities of my new life.

You ask me to write of my life in foreign countries while in earth life, Harold, but do you know that while I recall this event of my life here in general, to make mention of one particular instance known to you is quite a difficult task. In making the change called death, spirit retains memory in general of the events of life, but it is recalled in detail only as you mention or some particular circumstance brings it to mind, just as you recall your childhood days. Spirit life furnishes so much in the way of advanced conditions, surroundings and events, that the past becomes more indistinct as time advances. So it is quite difficult for me to carry out your request on this particular day, my boy, but the tie of relationship and love grows more intense as time advances. I watch over you with deepest interest and anxious thoughts, impressing you wherever and whenever I can find the need. Time will bring us in spiritual converse, and I shall then be able to come to you in ways of recognition far greater than references to earthly events could give.

We have the language of the soul; that is far reaching in understanding the evidence of identity. I love you, my boy, and shall come to (you), always, as best I can. Come to me in the silent hours of evening, when your thoughts turn to spiritual things, and I can give you much more in this way than through the influence of others.

With a mother's best devotion for her boy.

Adieu for the present,

Mother
Jane Thompson

APPENDIX G

———————>●<———————

"A Brief History of Camp Chesterfield, Indiana" by N. R. Heagerty

Spiritualism owes a vast debt of thanks to the Shakers who, from at least the year 1800 in America, had already been experiencing spirit rappings, visions, trances and physical phenomena, and in 1830 a major spiritual contact was recorded that told of an approaching "spiritual crisis" when a worldwide outpouring of spiritual gifts would occur, together with an extraordinary discovery of material wealth. The date set forth was 1848—the exact date of both the spirit rappings at the Fox cottage in Hydesville, New York—signaling the birth of Modern Spiritualism and the discovery of gold at Sutter's mill in California.

After the Civil War, camp meetings, or grove meetings as they were called, were being held regularly by the Spiritualists, one of the first of which was in Malden, Mass., in 1860. By the early 1880's, at least seventeen of these camps had sprung up all over the nation.

In Anderson, Indiana, in 1883, Dr. J. W. Westerfield and his wife, Mary, were encouraging free and progressive thinking, and Spiritualism. Over the next four years they slowly assembled an organization of people interested in their ideas and, by 1887, had drawn up what was to be the Constitution and By-Laws making this formed society an incorporated body, legally qualified to transact all business pertaining to the organization and the religion of Spiritualism, and, on October 22, 1888, with Dr. Westerfield as the elected president, the society was incorporated as the Indiana Association of Spiritualists.

In 1892, 34 acres of land in Union Township, Indiana, was purchased and is still today the same name as it was, The Chesterfield Spiritualist Camp.

The Chesterfield Camp, similar to Lily Dale, is a little town of Spiritualists. The only thing lacking, as compared with Lily Dale, is a post office. The grounds consist of an enormous common, or park, with beautiful swaying trees, leafy glens, statuary, fountains, beautiful flowers and stone benches, garden of prayer, and trail of religion.

Surrounding this area are six streets, three of which—its main thoroughfare—are Western Drive, Eastern Drive, and Grandview Drive. Along these tree-lined streets are many cottages and houses.

Outside many of these dwellings, similar to Lily Dale, are quaint little signs, which advertise what particular gifts the medium has. The grounds have an administration building, book store and gift shop, two hotels, The Hett Memorial Art Gallery, an impressive old wooden chapel and an enormous cathedral which seats 500 people or more. I was impressed to see a memorial plaque on the entrance wall to the cathedral dedicated to Etta Wriedt, one of the great American trumpet mediums. Those who are truly interested in the historical aspects of Spiritualism, owe it to themselves to go to Camp Chesterfield, especially to see and experience the Bangs Sisters' portraits, twenty-six of the glorious gems, displayed at the Hett Gallery.

APPENDIX H

———————›◊‹———————

"A Brief History of The Lily Dale Assembly, New York" by Ron Nagy

Lily Dale is the oldest community dedicated to the practice of the Spiritualist Religion. It is situated in Western, New York State, south of Buffalo, on the Upper Cassadaga Lake.

Founded in 1879 by Spiritualists, Free Thinkers and Liberals, a village was planned for the purpose of holding summer camp meetings for the study, practice and exchange of philosophical ideas. The Woman's Suffrage movement soon had a strong platform at Lily Dale. Susan B. Anthony, Reverend Anna Shaw, and Isabella Beecher Hooker were regular speakers. Within a short period of time a city of tents became an organized village of streets, with Victorian houses and 40 families living on the property year round.

Lily Dale did not have any one founder and did not just happen overnight. It all began in the year 1844—preceding by four years the Hydesville manifestations with the Fox Sisters. In the nearby village of Laona, William Johnson invited Dr. Moran, a mesmerist from Vermont, to lecture before a group of interested people. Mr. Johnson, the son of a minister, was the father of Marion Skidmore who eventually became a great leader for Spiritualism at Lily Dale.[23] At that time, Jeremiah Carter, physically enfeebled, had sought to be treated by Dr. Moran. Unfortunately, Dr. Moran had to leave before such could be applied. Mr. Johnson suggested that they try the mesmerism experiments demonstrated by the

---

[23] The Marion Skidmore Library is a 'must-see' for all those who are interested in Spiritualism, when visiting Lily Dale, and is situated on Cottage Row.

Vermont doctor. The results were startling. Mr. Carter became entranced, and an entity called Dr. Hedges spoke to the people who were present, giving messages from spirit and demonstrating the laying on of hands.

The advent of the Hydesville manifestations strengthened the purpose of the group and they termed themselves Spiritualists, Liberals and Free Thinkers. The group met regularly to discuss their beliefs and practice their healing and mediumship. Many great speakers and mediums had their early beginnings in Laona. In 1855 the First Spiritualist Society of Laona was formed.

In 1873, Willard Alden, who owned a farm and stagecoach stop along the east banks of the Cassadaga Lakes, had a visit from Jeremiah Carter, who insisted that spirit voices continuously kept urging him to go to Alden's farm and start a camp meeting. This was agreed upon with Mr. Alden for summer picnics and camp meetings. After Mr. Alden's transition, his heirs became dissatisfied with financial arrangements, so the Spiritualists in 1879 decided to purchase the land and move their location. Twenty acres of land was purchased, adjacent to the Alden farm, from John Fisher at the price of $1845. Mrs. Amelia Colby was asked to name the camp. Her spirit guide gave her the name of the Cassadaga Lake Free Association. In 1903 the name was changed to The City of Light and in 1906, The Lily Dale Assembly

- The first dedication service for Lily Dale was held under a cradle of boughs, known as the Bough House.
- The first speaker was Elizabeth Lowe Watson, a liberal and suffragette.
- An auditorium was built in 1883, and later remodeled in 1901; the seating capacity was twelve hundred.
- Preceding the auditorium, a children's Lyceum was formed and, in 1928, The Andrew Jackson Davis building for the Lyceum was built and gifted to Lily Dale by a group of prominent Spiritualists.
- A hotel was built in 1880. It was the Grand Hotel, renamed the Maplewood Hotel in 1903, and still stands today in full working glory.
- The first library was held in a tent in the park in 1886, and was then moved to the second floor of what is now named Assembly Hall. It is now the Marion Skidmore Library.
- The original Fox Cottage was moved from Hydesville, New York, a gift from Benjamin Bartlett, and placed in Lily Dale in 1915. Tragically the cottage burned to the ground in 1955.

- Lily Dale now owns more than one hundred sixty acres.
- The seasonal "camp" months are July and August, visited by thousands every year.

APPENDIX I

May Bangs on Trial & Article by Hermann Handrich, published in *Light*, 1909.

May Bangs Arrested

Since our article in *Light* was written, *The Progressive Thinker* of Chicago, dated August 7th, has come to hand, from which we learn that May Bangs has been arrested and that in her testimony when on trial, as reported in the *Inter Ocean*, and in the *Chicago Daily News*, she said: "I am not a Spiritualist. I am an artist. My pictures are made by the sun—hung in a window so that the sun can operate upon them with its rays, developing them."

Question: "Are there any spirits in the making of the picture?"

Answer: "The process is my own. Nobody would understand if I were to tell you how they are made."

Question: "Did you ever represent that you can draw these pictures or do anything else by the aid of spirit?"

Answer: "I suppose we all have a spirit," was the answer to this question.

Question: "Have you ever seen spirits of those departed?" asked Judge Scovel, interrupting.

Answer: "No sir."

The further hearing of the case was postponed until August 13th. Commenting upon the above *The Progressive Thinker* says:

There has been a great diversity of opinions in regard to the genuineness of the mediumship of the Bangs Sisters. The denial of Mrs. Bangs, under oath, that she is a Spiritualist, and her statement that the pictures are developed by sunlight, will put Spiritualists everywhere in a quandary in reference to them and their work. If their work is the result of spirit power, a great point could be gained by so declaring in court, and producing the same in the presence of judge and jury. At the Chesterfield Camp, on the rostrum, surrounded by a promiscuous audience, they obtained a 'spirit picture.' A judge and jury would act as favorably in producing good results as a promiscuous audience at a camp meeting.

APPENDIX J

———➤●◄———

"May Bangs Denial of Mediumship" by Hermann Hendrich

Spiritualists are greatly assisted nowadays in making their convictions known to the world, by the activity of prominent scientific men and of the daily press, formerly so hostile to the subject. It is, therefore, all the more to be deplored when Spiritualism receives a severe blow from one of its own adherents.

May Bangs, one of the Bangs Sisters, as reported recently, declared before a court of justice that she was not a medium. This fact reminds us of the alternate confessions and denials of so-called witches (mediums, as we should call them), during the days when they were hunted down, tortured and put to death; or of persons who falsely accuse themselves of crimes in order to be taken back to their homes at the expense of the authorities. As far as May Bangs herself is concerned, if she proclaimed herself a swindler, by the advice of her lawyer, instead of admitting that she was liable to the penalty for the practice of mediumship, she thus avoided protracted judicial proceedings and got off with a fine of twenty-five dollars for infringement of a city ordinance. It is not my purpose to break a lance on her behalf as an ill-advised person, but as a medium, and for the spirits who manifest their power through her.

Since this trial took place, my friend, Charles P. Cocks, an experienced investigator, went to the Camp Chesterfield to hold a sitting with the

Bangs Sisters, with whom he was already well acquainted. From his written and verbal account, which agrees with the experiences of my own, I take the following particulars.

As I had done in 1901, when the Bangs Sisters were on a visit to New York, Mr. Cocks placed some blank sheets of paper, bearing a private mark, in an envelope which he closed and sealed before going to the medium. He also, in his own room, wrote on separate pieces of paper questions addressed to his deceased first wife, his father, and brother. On arriving at the medium's home he placed these papers, folded, along with the sealed envelope, between two slates which he tied round with string and laid on the table, keeping them always within view. Almost immediately, May Bangs, who sat opposite to him, repeated the names of the three persons addressed, and in half an hour announced that the sitting was over. On separating the slates himself, Mr. Cocks noticed that the loose pieces of paper had disappeared, and on carefully opening the sealed envelope he found them—as he anticipated—inside, along with the sheets, originally blank, which he had enclosed in the envelope, and now which contained complete answers to his questions addressed to the departed. The replies were written with ink, ostensibly taken from the inkstand which was upon the table, but no pen was provided with which the messages could have been written. The writing must therefore be regarded as having been precipitated, not by the spirits who were addressed, but by the intelligence who acted as the medium's guide and as amanuensis to those wishing to communicate. All this is quite in accord with my own experiences in 1901, and I may add that, as regards the character of the writing itself and the formation of the letters, it is the exact facsimile of that obtained eight years ago.

On the following day Mr. Cocks had a sitting for a portrait of his deceased wife; this picture, like the one of his father which he had received some years before, must be regarded as a precipitated reproduction, in colors, of a portrait already existing. Apart from the fact that it was not a 'sitting for a portrait' in the ordinary sense of the word—the person represented not being visibly present—the result is as remarkable, in regard to the phenomena of its origin, as are the artistic gifts of the intelligence who, so to speak, handled the pencil.

My friend, Mr. Cocks, went to the medium at the appointed time, keeping carefully in his pocket a medallion containing a miniature photograph of his wife; this was not seen by May Bangs at any time. Out of a number of canvases stretched on frames ready for use by an artist, he chose one and marked it so as to obviate the possibility of substitution. It was set up in front of him, and the medium stood beside it. Contrary to May Bangs' assertion before the court, that the pictures were developed by the sun, the sky on that day was overcast, and yet in about twenty minutes the colored background was fully visible.

"It was a wonderful sight," continued my informant, "to watch the process and observe the changes which occurred after the outlines of the portrait had taken definite shape. A sweet smile animated the countenance and lighted up the naturally-colored eyes. I took the picture from the easel, and, while I held it in front of me and was looking at it, I perceived that the previously dark background was becoming lighter in places, and had assumed a pleasing bluish tint which remained permanently."

The portrait, like others I have compared with the originals, is an enlarged and perfectly sharp reproduction in colors, and the pictures take usually from thirty-five minutes to an hour to complete, and are sometimes produced in a darkened room. The execution would do credit to an accomplished artist, and in the ordinary way would require hours instead of as many minutes.

My object in writing the above is solely to show that Miss May Bangs, if the newspaper reports are trustworthy, rendered herself guilty before the magistrate of a false and cowardly denial of the mediumistic gifts bestowed on her by nature.

In this writer and editor's view, May Bangs was a victim of her own fear, and chose to stay silent about her gifts, and by so doing, incurred the wrath of her own comrades. I feel, in my humble opinion, although 115 years hence, that she should have stood her ground, and defended the honorable name of Spiritualism and mediumship. It did not, though, tarnish the power and legitimacy of her mediumistic gifts. She should have offered to demonstrate a precipitated portrait for the judge and jury right then and there, with blank canvases and using one of the courtroom windows and table, etc. That would have been a momentous and historic moment for the Spiritualists the world over if there ever was one. The question will always remain whether she was acting on the advice of her attorney and fell to that pressure, or chose the other route of fear.

APPENDIX K

—————>●●<—————

Spiritualism by N. Riley Heagerty

> "...Behold, I Have Set Before Thee an Open Door, and No Man Can
> Shut It"
>
> - REVELATIONS-3-8

I have met many materialistically minded individuals over the years
who believe that who a person was what they said, and what they
had accomplished in this life, and the memory of them, which stays
with those who are still here, is all there is to that individual after they
leave this world. I have never for an instant believed in that theory even
before my research into mediumship and spirits began so long ago. My
journey began with the loss of someone dear and close to me, and that
too can be the starting point for many individuals looking for answers
to life after death and spirit communication. I consider myself extremely fortunate to have discovered so many amazing works involving the
teachings of Spiritualism. It has liberated my mind. This discovery led
to an interest in Shamanism, and other great avenues of thought and
perspectives concerning the Universe and our place in it.

I would like to share with you the words of Alfred Russel Wallace,
the famous naturalist and co-discoverer, along with Charles Darwin,
of the principles of evolution. He wrote these words in 1878 and 1900:

> I prefer to rest the claims of Spiritualism on its moral uses. I would
> point to the thousands it has convinced of the reality of another world,
> to the many it has led to devote their lives to works of philanthropy,

to the eloquence and the poetry it has given us, and to the grand doctrines of an ever-progressive future state which it teaches. *Those who will examine its literature will acknowledge these facts.*

And, from *A Defense of Modern Spiritualism* he said:

The subject, of which I have here endeavored to sketch the outlines in a few pages which may perhaps be read when larger volumes would lie unopened, is far too wide and too important for this mode of treatment to do any justice to it. I have been obliged entirely to leave out all mention of the historical proofs of similar phenomena occurring in unbroken succession from the earliest ages to the present day. I could not refer to the numbers of scientific and medical men, who have been convinced of its truth, but have not made public their belief. But I claim to show cause for investigation; to have proved that it is not a subject that can any longer be contemptuously sneered at as unworthy of a moment's inquiry. I feel myself so confident of the truth and objective reality of many of the facts, that I would stake the whole question on the opinion of any man of science desirous of arriving at the truth, if he would only devote two or three hours a week for a few months to the examination of the phenomena, before pronouncing an opinion; for I again repeat, not a single individual that I have heard of, has done this without becoming convinced of the reality of these phenomena. I maintain, therefore, finally that—whether we consider the vast number and high character of its converts, the immense accumulation and the authenticity of its facts, or the noble doctrine of a future state which it has elaborated— the so-called supernatural, as developed in the phenomenon of modern Spiritualism, is an experimental science, the study of which must add greatly to our knowledge of man's true nature and highest interests.

It will be seen that the phenomenon of Spiritualism is no mere 'psychological 'curiosity, no mere indication of some hitherto unknown 'law of nature, 'but that it is a science of vast extent, having the widest, the most important, and the most practical issues, and as such should enlist the sympathies alike of moralists, philosophers, and politicians, and all who have at heart the improvement of society and the permanent elevation of human nature. I would ask all to dwell upon the long series of facts in human history that the phenomenon of Spiritualism explains, and on the noble and satisfying theory of a future life that it unfolds.

Through the voice mediumship of Mrs. Emily S. French in my first book, *The French Revelation*, a spirit, when commenting on the theory of "justice" as it might pertain to those who have led questionable or nefarious lives on earth, said, in his own voice, which emanated from seemingly thin air about three feet above the medium: "The justice which meets every soul on the threshold of the afterlife is *Terrible in its Completeness...*" I have often pondered on the indescribable largeness of that statement and it seems to be in alignment with the following words which I found.

The famous spirit guide of Maurice Barbanell, Silver Birch, had this to say concerning the power of Natural Law:

> Sowing and reaping are part of the Natural Law, which I wish was accepted by more people. It is the cultivation of the fruits of the earth that you learn how inexorable are the laws of the Great Spirit. He who lives close to the soil and sees the operation of nature's law begins to appreciate the divine handiwork and to realize something of the Mind, which has planned all in its orderly sequence.
>
> That which is garnered is that which has been sown. The seed is always true to its type. You cannot grow the seed of a potato and expect that a lettuce will grow. Always what has been sown will follow unswervingly the dictate of the Natural Law. And what is true in that realm of nature is equally true in the realm of human life and activity.
>
> He who lives selfishly must reap the results of selfishness. He who sins must reap the result of sin. He who is intolerant, bigoted or selfish will reap the results of intolerance, bigotry and selfishness. The law is inexorable; the law is immutable. There is no religious exercise; there is no hymn, no prayer, no sacred book that can *interpose and alter the sequence of cause and effect.*
>
> The effect follows cause with methodical and mechanical certainty, and no one has the power, be he called priest or layman, to interfere with or modify by one hairbreadth this sequence....the soul of every individual registers indelibly all the results of earthly life.

These facts of life, which appeal to common sense, breed conscience and that is what can change the world. It is never too late.

Namaste

APPENDIX L

———————

Suggested Reading List: Physical Mediumship

These titles, many of which are great, rare classics, I highly recommend to those interested in the subject of Physical Mediumship.

Bailey, D. E. *Thoughts from the Inner Life*. Colby & Rich, 1886.

Barry, Catherine. *Experiences in Spiritualism: A record of Extraordinary Phenomena Witnessed Through the Most Powerful Mediums*, James Burns, London, 1876

Barbanell, Maurice. *The Trumpet Shall Sound*, Rider & Co., London, 1933. *This is Spiritualism*, Spiritualist Press, 1959, 1967, London.

Bowers, Dr. Edwin F. *The Phenomena of the Séance Room*, Rider & Co., London, 1930

Brace, Josephine M. *The Descending Light*, John Higgins Press, Chicago, 1922

Bradley, Dennis H. *The Wisdom of the Gods*, 1925, *Towards the Stars*, 1928, T. Werner Laurie Ltd., London

Britt, Coleen O. *Byron-Station to Station*, Dale News, Inc., Lily Dale, New York/London, 1941

Chapman, Clive. *The Blue Room*, The Psychic Book Club Ltd., London, 1927

Coates, James. *Photographing the Invisible*, L. N. Fowler & Co., London, 1911

Cook, Mrs. Cecil M. *The Voice Triumphant*, Alfred A. Knopf, New York, 1931

Conacher, Douglas. *Chapters from Experience*, Frederick Mullen Co., London, 1973.

Crane, H. Montague. *Spirit Voices*. Alex Wildey Ltd., Christchurch, New Zealand, 1931.

Daiches, Belle Turner. *Adventures in Survival*, Aries Press-Publishers, Chicago, 1949

Drouet, Bessis Clark. *Station Astral*, G. P. Putnam's Sons, New York/ London, 1932.

Duncan, Rev. V.G. *Proof*, G. P. Putnam's Sons, New York, 1932.

Eddy, Sherwood. *You Will Survive After Death*, Clark Pub. Co., Evanston, Ill., 1950.

John S. Farmer. *Twixt Two Worlds*, The Psychological Press, London, 1886.

Findlay, J. Arthur. *On the Edge of the Etheric*, 1931/*Where Two Worlds Meet*, 1951/*The Way of Life*, 1953, Psychic Press Limited/The Headquarters Pub. Co., Ltd., London.

Fitzsimons, F. W. *Opening the Psychic Door*, Hutchinson & Co., Ltd., London, 1933.

Heagerty, N. Riley. *The French Revelation*, 2000/2001, White Crow Books.

King, Dr. John. *Dawn of the Awakened Mind*, James A. McCann Co., New York, 1920.

Moore, Vice Admiral W. Usborne. *Glimpses of the Next State*, 1911, The Voices, 1913, *White Crow Books* (whitecrowbooks.com)

Nagy, Ron. *Precipitated Spirit Paintings*, 2006, Slate Writing; Invisible *Intelligence*, 2009, Galde Press, Minnesota.

Nichols, T. L., M. D. *A Biography of the Brothers Davenport*, Saunders, Otley & Co., London, 1864

Perriman, A. E. *Broadcasting from Beyond*, Ebenezer Baylis & Son, Ltd., London, 1952.

Remmers, John H. *Is Death the End? 1928, The Great Reality, 1967,* Ebenezer Baylis & Son, Ltd., London.

Robertson, James. *Spiritualism, The Open Door to the Unseen Universe,* L. N. Fowler & Co., 1908.

Robertson, F.T. *Celestial Voices,* H. H. Graves, London, 1945.

Sewell, May Wright. *Neither Dead Nor Sleeping,* John M. Watkins, London, 1921.

APPENDIX M

———⇒●⇐———

Articles & Sources.

Atchinson Little Globe, 1881
Chicago Daily Tribune, 1891
Los Angeles Times, 1895
The Sunflower, 1905
Chicago Daily Tribune, 1905
The National Spiritualist, 1940
Chesterfield Lives, Camp Chesterfield, 1986
The Bangs Sisters and their Precipitated Spirit Portraits
Compiled by Irene Swann, Hett Memorial Art Gallery & Museum, 1969
Photographing the Invisible
By James Coates, London, 1911
Light of Truth, 1896-97
The Sunflower, Bangs Sisters Advertisement, 1900
The Lily Dale Chronicle, 1900-20
Slate Writing
Invisible Intelligence
By Ron Nagy, 2009
The Facts of Psychic Science
& Philosophy by A. Campbell Holms, 1969
Neither Dead Nor Sleeping
May Wright Sewell, London, 1921
Tribune Republican/The Sunflower, 1901
What I Saw at Casadaga Lake/Seybert Commission Report, Addendum

By A. B. Richmond, 1888
The Encyclopedia of Psychic Science
By Nandor Fodor, 1966
Glimpses of the Next State
W. Usborne Moore, London, 1911
Marguerite Hunter
By Marguerite Hunter- in Spirit
C. H. Horine, 1894 & *Slate Writing with Lizzie Bangs*, Noah's Ark Society, 2003, by N. Riley Heagerty
Through the Valley of the Shadow and Beyond
By Rose M. Carson-in Spirit, 1908
Proceedings of The American Society of Psychical Research, 1901
Annals of Psychic Science, 1910
The Spirit Portrait Mystery: Its Final Solution
By David P. Abbott, Chicago, 1913
Spirit Precipitated Paintings
By Ron Nagy, 2006
Light, Hereward Carrington, 1911
A Card from the Bangs Sisters
Chicago (Newspaper), 1891
Chicago Daily Tribune, 1890's
State of Indiana Sworn Affidavit
Published in The Bangs Sisters and their Spirit Precipitated Portraits, ibid.
The Sunflower, 1905
The National Spiritualist, 1940.
Light of Truth, 1898
Article, *Shows Spirit Picture,* by Charles Peck, 1900's from *Precipitated Spirit Paintings,* Nagy, ibid.
The Sunflower: Two Fine Portraits, 1905
Dawn of the Awakened Mind,
By John S. King, New York, 1920
Nineteenth Century Miracles, Emma Hardinge Britten, 1884
Noah's Ark Review, The Newsletter, England, January-November, 1997
The Zerdin Phenomenal, Buzzsheet, England, October, 2006

Lily Dale Chronicle 1915.

The Roof Tree
Lily Dalights

"Mrs. Bangs and her expansive smile has arrived."

This is the last known information printed on the
Bangs Sisters that we know of.

Lizzie passed away in 1920, and May in 1917.

Paperbacks also available from
White Crow Books

Elsa Barker—*Letters from a Living Dead Man*
ISBN 978-1-907355-83-7

Elsa Barker—*War Letters from
the Living Dead Man*
ISBN 978-1-907355-85-1

Elsa Barker—*Last Letters from
the Living Dead Man*
ISBN 978-1-907355-87-5

Richard Maurice Bucke—
Cosmic Consciousness
ISBN 978-1-907355-10-3

Stafford Betty—
The Imprisoned Splendor
ISBN 978-1-907661-98-3

Stafford Betty—
*Heaven and Hell Unveiled: Updates
from the World of Spirit.*
ISBN 978-1-910121-30-6

Ineke Koedam—
*In the Light of Death: Experiences on
the threshold between life and death*
ISBN 978-1-910121-48-1

Arthur Conan Doyle with Simon Parke—
Conversations with Arthur Conan Doyle
ISBN 978-1-907355-80-6

Meister Eckhart with Simon Parke—
Conversations with Meister Eckhart
ISBN 978-1-907355-18-9

D. D. Home—*Incidents in my Life Part 1*
ISBN 978-1-907355-15-8

Mme. Dunglas Home; edited, with an
Introduction, by Sir Arthur Conan
Doyle—*D. D. Home: His Life and Mission*
ISBN 978-1-907355-16-5

Edward C. Randall—
Frontiers of the Afterlife
ISBN 978-1-907355-30-1

Rebecca Ruter Springer—
Intra Muros: My Dream of Heaven
ISBN 978-1-907355-11-0

Leo Tolstoy, edited by Simon
Parke—*Forbidden Words*
ISBN 978-1-907355-00-4

Erlendur Haraldsson and
Loftur Gissurarson—
*Indridi Indridason: The Icelandic
Physical Medium*
ISBN 978-1-910121-50-4

Goerge E. Moss—
*Earth's Cosmic Ascendancy: Spirit
and Extraterrestrials Guide us
through Times of Change*
ISBN 978-1-910121-28-3

Steven T. Parsons and Callum E. Cooper—
Paracoustics: Sound & the Paranormal
ISBN 978-1-910121-32-0

L. C. Danby—
*The Certainty of Eternity: The Story
of Australia's Greatest Medium*
ISBN 978-1-910121-34-4

Madelaine Lawrence —
*The Death View Revolution: A
Guide to Transpersonal Experiences
Surrounding Death*
ISBN 978-1-910121-37-5

Zofia Weaver—
*Other Realities?: The enigma of
Franek Kluski's mediumship*
ISBN 978-1-910121-39-9

Roy L. Hill—
*Psychology and the Near-Death
Experience: Searching for God*
ISBN 978-1-910121-42-9

Tricia. J. Robertson —
*"Things You Can do When You're Dead!: True
Accounts of After Death Communication"*
ISBN 978-1-908733-60-3

Tricia. J. Robertson —
*More Things you Can do When You're
Dead: What Can You Truly Believe?*
ISBN 978-1-910121-44-3

Jody Long—
*God's Fingerprints: Impressions
of Near-Death Experiences*
ISBN 978-1-910121-05-4

Leo Tolstoy with Simon Parke—
Conversations with Tolstoy
ISBN 978-1-907355-25-7

www.ingramcontent.com/pod-product-compliance
Lightning Source LLC
Chambersburg PA
CBHW070030100426
42740CB00013B/2650